Professor Barclay was a distinguished scholar, an exceptionally gifted preacher and a regular broadcaster. His writings for the *British Weekly* were very popular and for twenty years from 1950 a full page every week was given to them. From 1963 until 1974 he was Professor of Divinity and Biblical Criticism at Glasgow University. He was a Member of the Advisory Committee working on the New English Bible and also a Member of the Apocrypha Panel of Translators. In 1975 he was appointed a Visiting Professor at the University of Strathclyde for a period of three years where he lectured on Ethics, and in the same year – jointly with the Rev. Professor James Stewart – he received the 1975 Citation from the American theological organization The Upper Room; the first time it has been awarded outside America. His extremely popular *Bible Study Notes* using his own translation of the New Testament have achieved a world-wide sale.

Professor Barclay died in January 1978.

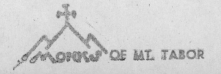

MONKS OF MT. TABOR

WILLIAM
BARCLAY

Plain
People
Look at the
Beatitudes

ABINGDON PRESS / Nashville

PLAIN PEOPLE LOOK AT THE BEATITUDES

Copyright © 1965 by William Barclay. All rights reserved.
Published originally in Great Britain by William Collins Sons
& Co., Ltd.
Reprinted in the U.S. by Abingdon Press,
by permission of Harper Collins Publishers.

Published by Abingdon Press in 1993 as an Abingdon Classic.
Previously published as *The Plain Man Looks at the Beatitudes*,
under ISBN 0-00-626937-9.

No part of this work may be reproduced or transmitted in any
form or by any means, electronic or mechanical, including
photocopying and recording, or by any information storage or
retrieval system, except as may be expressly permitted by the
1976 Copyright Act or in writing from the publisher. Requests
for permission should be addressed in writing to Abingdon
Press, 201 Eighth Avenue South, P.O. Box 801, Nashville,
TN 37203.

93 94 95 96 97 98 99 00 01 02—10 9 8 7 6 5 4 3 2 1

Library of Congress Cataloging-in-Publication Data

Barclay, William, 1907–1978.
    [Plain man looks at the Beatitudes]
    Plain people look at the Beatitudes / William Barclay.
    p.   cm.
    Originally published: The plain man looks at the
Beatitudes.
London : Collins, 1963.
    ISBN 0-687-31550-6 (alk. paper)
    1. Beatitudes. I. Title.
BT382.B3692   1993
241.5′3—dc20   92-35214
                                                        CIP

MANUFACTURED IN THE UNITED STATES OF AMERICA

CONTENTS

AUTHOR'S NOTE

The chapters of this book have a double origin. In the first place, they represent the substance of lectures given over the years to my students in Trinity College, Glasgow.

In lecturing over the years a man uses many sources, and in the end he so integrates material into his own lectures that he forgets what is his own and what he has borrowed from other sources. I hope that if I have, in these chapters, failed to acknowledge any borrowings, the people from whom I have borrowed will understand and forgive.

In the second place, these chapters originally appeared as a series of articles in the *Preachers' Quarterly*. I have to thank the editor of that magazine for, in the first place, allowing me the courtesy of his columns and, in the second place, allowing me to issue these chapters as a book.

The author and publisher thank the following for kind permission to quote from the works mentioned: The Society of Authors as the literary representative of the Estate of the late A. E. Housman, and Messrs Jonathan Cape Ltd., publishers of A. E. Housman's *Collected Poems*; Hodder & Stoughton Ltd., *The Best of Studdert Kennedy*; G. Bell & Sons Ltd., Aristophanes' *Plutus* translated by B. B. Rogers.

CHAPTER I

THE ESSENCE OF THE ESSENCE

For most people the Sermon on the Mount is the essence of the Christian faith and life; and equally for most people the Beatitudes are the essence of the Sermon on the Mount. It is therefore not too much to say that the Beatitudes are the essence of the essence of the Christian way of life.

In this case the findings of the New Testament scholarship have confirmed that which the ordinary person instinctively feels. The detailed study of the Sermon on the Mount confirms the conviction that it is indeed the central document of the Christian faith. Three times in his introduction to it Matthew makes that clear (Matthew 5.1,2):

And seeing the multitudes Jesus went up into a mountain; and, when he was set, his disciples came unto him; and he opened his mouth and taught them.

i. *When he was set* means *when he had sat down.* Often a Jewish Rabbi would talk to his disciples when he was walking along the road with them, or when he was strolling in some city square or colonnade; but when he was teaching, as we might put it, officially, he always sat to do so. This was the Jewish attitude of official teaching. In the Synagogue the preacher sat to deliver the sermon. We still talk of a professor's *chair*, which was the chair in which he sat to deliver his lectures to his students. When the Pope makes an official announcement he speaks *ex cathedra*, seated in his papal throne. From this introduction Matthew means us to see that what follows is no chance teaching given in the by-going; it is no pleasant discourse given in the passing; it is the official teaching of Jesus. It is Jesus telling his disciples the very essence of what he came to say.

ii. The phrase *he opened his mouth* is more than an elaborate or poetical way of saying *he said*. It has certain overtones and implications.

a. It is regularly used to introduce any weighty, grave and important utterance. It is the phrase of the great occasion. It is used, for instance, of the utterance of an oracle, which the hearer will neglect at his peril. In the New Testament itself this phrase is used on two very significant occasions. It is used of Philip expounding the meaning of scripture to the Ethiopian eunuch (Acts 8.35). Philip was giving the Ethiopian an authoritative exposition of the message of scripture regarding Jesus. It is used of Peter, when, after the conversion of the Roman centurion. Cornelius, he expounded the epoch-making discovery that the gospel was for the Gentiles also (Acts 10.34). This phrase is regularly the preface to some pronouncement of the greatest weight and importance, and it is the warning that there is something to follow which must not be lightly disregarded.

b. It is used of an utterance of calculated courage. A phrase very closely kin to it is used by the great Greek orator Isocrates in the last speech he ever made, his final witness and testimonial to the glory of Athens. On that occasion he says that he is moved to use the greatest freedom of speech, whatever the consequence may be, and to *remove the curb from his tongue* (*Panathenaicus* 96). It is used of a speaker who will shrink from saying nothing that ought to be said, and who will speak, fearless of anything that men may do to him.

c. It is used of an utterance in which there are no reservations, in which nothing is kept back, and in which the whole truth is told and the whole heart opened. In Aeschylus' *Prometheus Vinctus,* when Io asks for information about the future, Prometheus answers: "I will tell thee plainly all that thou art fain to know . . . even as it is right *to open the lips* to friends." The whole atmosphere of the phrase is the opening of the mind and the heart in such a way that nothing is kept back.

By using this phrase of Jesus Matthew warns us that there is to follow an utterance of the greatest weight and importance, an utterance in which no cautious and prudential motives of safety will keep the speaker from telling the truth, an utterance in which mind and heart are opened and in which nothing is kept back.

iii. Matthew says that Jesus *taught* his disciples. In Greek there are two past tenses of the verb. There is the *aorist* which describes one completed action in past time. There is the *imperfect* which describes repeated and habitual action in past time. "He shut the door behind him," would be expressed by an aorist tense; "it was his habit always to shut doors behind him," would be expressed by an imperfect tense. The tense in Matthew's introduction is the imperfect tense. Therefore in what follows we are to see, not simply a statement made by Jesus on one occasion, but the substance of all that he habitually and repeatedly taught his disciples. We are not to see here only one sermon; we are to see the summary of the teaching which Jesus continually and consistently gave to his disciples. It is therefore nothing more than the actual fact to say that the Sermon on the Mount is the essence of the teaching of Jesus.

All Matthew's phrases converge to show how essential to the teaching of Jesus the material which is to follow is. It therefore follows that the study of the Beatitudes is one of the most important studies to which the Christian, or the man who wishes to find out the meaning of Christianity, can devote himself.

CHAPTER II

THE DIVINE BLISS

The Authorised Version prints the Beatitudes as statements; but in each case it prints the *are* in italic print, which is the conventional sign that there is no corresponding word in the Greek text. In the Greek there is no verb in any of the Beatitudes, which means that the Beatitudes are not statements, but exclamations. They reproduce in Greek a form of expression which is very common in Hebrew, especially in the Psalms. Hebrew has an exclamatory word *ashere,* which means: "O the bliss of . . ." So the Psalmist says: "O the bliss of the man who walks not in the counsel of the ungodly . . . but whose delight is in the law of the Lord" (Psalm 1. 1). "O the bliss of the man to whom the Lord does not impute iniquity, and in whose spirit there is no guile" (Psalm 32. 2). "O the bliss of the man whom thou chastenest, O Lord, and teachest him out of thy law" (Psalm 94. 12). This is the form of expression which each of the Beatitudes represents; each of them is an exclamation beginning: "O the bliss of . . . !" That is to say that the Beatitudes are not promises of future happiness; they are congratulations on present bliss. They are not statements and prophecies of what is one day going to happen to the Christian in some other world; they are affirmations of the bliss into which the Christian can enter even here and now. That is not to say that this bliss will not reach its perfection and its completion, when some day the Christian enters into the nearer presence of his Lord; but it is to say that even here and now the foretaste and the experience of that bliss is meant to be part of the Christian life.

And what is that bliss? The word which is translated *blessed* is the word *makarios,* which in its older form in Greek was *makar.* The characteristic of that word is that properly it describes a bliss which belongs only to the gods. Although the word lost something of its greatness and came to be used in a wider and a looser sense, the fact remains that in Greek thought only the gods were truly *hoi makarioi,* the Blessed Ones. In the New Testament itself God himself is twice described by this word. In the pastoral Epistles we read of the glorious gospel of the *blessed* God, and God is called the *blessed* and only Potentate, the King of kings and Lord of lords (I Timothy 1. 11; 6. 15). Two further uses of this word will make its meaning clearer yet. It is used of the Blessed Isles, the place of perfect happiness to which the blessed go, the place where pain and sorrow and hunger and all distress are gone, and where there is a serenity and a joy which nothing can touch (Pindar, *Olympians* 2. 70). Again, Herodotus uses this word to describe an oasis in the desert (Herodotus 3. 26). All around there is the desert with its sand and its thirst and its agony of body and of spirit; in the oasis there is shade and shelter, and peace for the weary traveller. F. W. Boreham quotes a tradition that Cyprus was in ancient times called *He Makaria,* the Blessed Isle, because the climate was so perfect, the soil so fertile, and the natural resources so complete, that he who dwelt in Cyprus never needed to go beyond it to find his perfect happiness and all his needs supplied.

Here we have our answer. The promised bliss is nothing less than the blessedness of God. Through Jesus Christ the Christian comes to share in the very life of God. The bliss of the Beatitudes is another expression of what John calls Eternal Life. Eternal life is *zoe aionios;* in Greek there is only one person in the universe to whom the word *aionios* may properly be applied, and that person is God. Eternal life is nothing less than the life of God, and it is a share in that life that Jesus Christ offers to men.

If that is so, it means that the Christian bliss is independent of outward circumstances; like the island of Cyprus, it has within itself all it needs for perfect happiness. It is independent of all the chances and the changes of life. That, indeed, is why happiness is not a good name for it. Happiness has in it the root *hap,* which means *chance;* and happiness is something which is dependent on the chances and alterations of this life; but the Christian bliss is the bliss of the life of God, and is, therefore, the joy that no man can take from us.

If this Christian bliss is the bliss of the blessedness of God, we will not be surprised to find that it completely reverses the world's standards. O the bliss of the poor! O the bliss of the sorrowful! O the bliss of the hungry and thirsty! O the bliss of the persecuted! These are startling contradictions of the world's standards; these are sayings which no man could hear for the first time

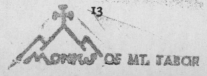

without a shock of amazement. Deissmann said of the Beatitudes: "They are not quiet stars, but flashes of lightning, followed by a thunder of surprise and amazement." But when we look at the Beatitudes carefully, we see that they are very closely interwoven into a threefold bliss.

There is the bliss which comes when a man recognises his deepest need, and discovers where that need can be supplied. There can be three periods in any life. There can be the period when a man lives placidly and in a kind of drab mediocrity, because he knows nothing better. There can be a period of restless dissatisfaction and even of mental agony, when something makes him realize that there is an unidentified something missing in his life. And there can be the period into which there enters a new joy and a new depth into life, because a man has found that wherein his newly discovered need can be supplied. So there is bliss for the man who discovers his own poverty, for the man who becomes sorrowfully aware of his own sin, and for the man who hungers and thirsts for a righteousness which he knows is not in him.

There is the bliss of living the Christian life. There is the bliss which comes in living in mercy, in meekness, in purity of heart, and in the making of peace. These were the qualities of Jesus Christ himself, and he who follows in the steps of Jesus Christ knows the joy of the Christian life.

There is the bliss of suffering for Jesus Christ. Long ago Plato said that the good man will always choose to suffer wrong rather than to do wrong. Herein is the bliss of loyalty, and there is the deepest of all satisfactions in loyalty, even when loyalty costs all that a man has to give.

On the face of it, it might look as if the Beatitudes looked for bliss all in the wrong places; but when we think again we can see that the way of the Beatitudes is the only way to bliss.

CHAPTER III

THE BLISS OF THE DESTITUTE

Blessed are the poor in spirit, for theirs is the kingdom of heaven (MATTHEW 5. 3).

Jesus could hardly have produced a more startling beginning to his Beatitudes. And Luke has it even more uncompromisingly: Blessed be ye poor, for yours is the kingdom of God (Luke 6. 20). There are very few people who would agree that poverty is a blessing, or that there is any bliss to be found in destitution. Dr. Johnson lays it down: "Resolve not to be poor . . . Poverty is a great enemy to human happiness; it certainly destroys liberty, and it makes some virtues impracticable, and others extremely difficult." Most people would speak of the curse of poverty rather than of the blessing of poverty.

The more closely we examine this saying, the more startling it becomes. The word which is used in the Greek for *poor* is *ptochos,* which is the adjective to describe, not one who is simply poor, but one who is completely destitute. The Greeks connected *ptochos* with the verb *ptossein* which means *to crouch* or *to cower,* and which Homer uses to describe the *cringing* of a suppliant beggar (Homer, *Odyssey* 17. 227). Aeschylus shows us Cassandra stripping off the insignia of a

16

prophetess, and deciding to become a vagrant, *begging* gipsy (Aeschylus, *Agamemnon* 1274). When the wretched Oedipus had lost his kingdom, and everything with it, Sophocles describes him as reduced to *penury*, a man in exile and a beggar (Sophocles, *Oedipus Coloneus* 444. 751). Herodotus uses the word *ptochos* to describe a man, who was well-born and who had once been rich, and who is reduced to begging scraps of food from the soldiers to keep body and soul together (Herodotus 3. 14). In the Code of Justinian the corresponding noun *ptocheia* means *poor relief*. For the man who is *ptochos* there is nothing left in this world but the poor-house.

But Greek has two words for *poor*. The second is the word *penes*, which describes the man who has nothing superfluous, the man who has to work for his living, the man who has to satisfy his needs with the work of his hands. Such a man is *autodiakonos*, under the necessity of serving himself. Socrates frequently described himself as *penes*, because he had given so much time to the gods that he had no time to build up a lucrative career for himself (Plato, *Apology* 23 C). But Socrates was in no danger of imminent starvation, however frugal his life might be. But the word *ptochos*, the other word for *poor*, describes, not the man who has nothing superfluous, but the man who has nothing at all. In the *Plutus* of Aristophanes *Penia*, Poverty, is one of the characters, and she herself draws a distinction between the man who is *penes* and the man who is *ptochos*, between the man who is poor and frugal and the man who is destitute and a beggar (Aristophanes, *Plutus* 550-554; Rogers' translation):

But the life I allot to my people is not, nor shall be
    so full of distresses.
'Tis a beggar (*ptochos*) alone who has naught of his
    own, nor even an obol (i.e. a penny piece)
    possesses.
My poor man (*penes*) 'tis true, has to scrape and to
    screw, and his work he must never be slack in;
There'll be no superfluity found in his cot; but then
    there will nothing be lacking.

In this Beatitude Tertullian alters the translation of
the Vulgate (*Against Marcion* 4. 14). The Vulgate
has: "Blessed are the *pauperes,* that is, the *poor.*"
Tertullian alters it to: "Blessed are the *mendici,* that
is, the beggars."

In the eyes of the Greek there was something wretched
and pitiable and even shameful in this word *ptochos*.
In his legislation for the ideal state Plato banishes the
ptochos from the community. "There shall be no
beggar (*ptochos*) in our state; and, if anyone attempts
to beg . . . he shall be driven across the border by the
country stewards, to the end that the land may be wholly
purged by such a creature" (Plato, *Laws* 936 C). In
the Gospels themselves the word *ptochos* describes the
wretched Lazarus who was daily dumped to beg at the
gate of the rich man (Luke 16. 20, 21); the widow whose
total possessions amounted to two mites, half a farthing
(Mark 12. 42, 43); the vagrants who were to be brought
in from the highways and the hedges to be the
unexpected guests at the banquet of the king (Luke
14. 21). It is by the word *ptochos* that James describes

the poor man who is contemptuously pushed aside to give the rich man the place of prominence and honour (James 2. 2, 3).

Milligan rightly remarks that the word *ptochos* was always used in a bad sense, until it was ennobled by the gospel. It would be difficult to find a word which to pagan ears had more of humiliation in it than the word *ptochos*.

But this is only one side of the picture. Jesus did not speak in Greek; he spoke in Aramaic; and his thought and language had their source and origin in the Old Testament. *Ptochos* represents the Old Testament word *ani,* which is generally translated *poor,* but which had acquired a special and distinctive meaning in the devotional literature of the Old Testament. The word *ani* underwent a four stage development of meaning in Hebrew. i. Originally it meant *poor* in the literal sense of the term. ii. A poor man is a man who has no power, no prestige, no influence to defend himself against the insults and the assaults of the world. iii. Such a man will be downtrodden and oppressed, and pushed to the wall in the competitive society of this world. iv. But such a man, in spite of everything, may retain his integrity and his devotion, and may be convinced that it is better to be humiliated with God than it is to be prosperous with the world. Hence the word *ani* came finally to describe the poor, humble, faithful man, who has no help on earth, and who in perfect trust has wholly committed himself to God.

In this sense the word *ani* becomes characteristic of the Psalms. "This poor man (*ani*) cried, and the Lord heard him, and saved him out of his troubles" (Psalm 34. 6; cp. Psalm 35. 10; 40. 17; 72. 2).

So, then, when we bring together the Greek and the Hebrew background of this word *poor*, we see that it describes the man who has fully realized his own inadequacy, his own worthlessness, and his own destitution, and who has put his whole trust in God. It describes the man who has realized that by himself life is impossible but that with God all things are possible; the man who has become so dependent on God that he has become independent of everything else in the universe.

This Beatitude has in it a whole attitude to life. It has in it three basic truths about life.

i. It means that the way to power lies through the realization of helplessness; that the way to victory lies through the admission of defeat; that the way to goodness lies through the confession and the acknowledgment of sin. Herein is an essential truth which runs through all life. If a man is ill, the first necessity is that he should admit and recognise that he is ill, and that then he should seek for a cure in the right place. The way to knowledge begins with the admission of ignorance. The one man who can never learn is the man who thinks that he knows everything already. Plato said: "He is the wisest man who knows himself to be very ill-qualified for the attainment of wisdom." Quintilian, the Roman master of oratory, said of certain of his students: "They would doubtless have become excellent scholars, if they had not been so fully persuaded of their own scholarship." This Beatitude affirms the basic fact that the first necessity towards the attainment of fulness of life is a sense of need.

ii. The second thing which this Beatitude does is to make a complete revaluation of what constitutes wealth. It lays it down that true wealth can never consist in the possession of things. The man who has nothing but money with which to meet life is a poverty-stricken man. The essential characteristic of material things is their insecurity. There is none of them which cannot be lost, often all unexpectedly and without warning. It was this fact of life which produced Solon's grim saying. Solon was visiting Croesus of Sardis. He saw Croesus in all his wealth and absolutely confident in the future. "Call no man happy," said Solon grimly, "until he is dead." This Beatitude lays it down that the man who has put his trust in that which his own skill or ingenuity can acquire has put his trust in the wrong place, and that before life ends he will make the tragic discovery that he has done so.

iii. The third thing which this Beatitude teaches is that the way to independence lies through dependence, and the way to freedom lies through surrender. If ever a man is to be independent of the chances and the changes of life, that independence must come from his complete dependence on God. If ever a man is to know true freedom, that freedom must come through complete surrender to God.

This Beatitude lays down that the way to the bliss which the world can neither give nor take away lies through the recognition of our own need, and the conviction that that need can be met, when we commit to God in perfect trust.

Each of the Beatitudes contains, not only an affirmation, but also a promise. " Blessed are the poor in spirit ", says this Beatitude, and then it goes on to promise, " for theirs is the kindom of heaven." What, then, is the meaning of this promise which is made to the poor in spirit? What is the kingdom of heaven?

We must first note that the two phrases *the kingdom of heaven* and *the kingdom of God* mean exactly the same thing. In the Gospels Matthew almost invariably speaks of *the kingdom of heaven,* and Mark and Luke almost invariably speak of *the kingdom of God.* The reason for the difference in practice lies in this. Such was the reverence of a strict and orthodox Jew that he would never, if he could avoid it, take the name of God upon his lips. He always, if possible, used some periphrasis to avoid actually uttering the name of God. It is very natural that by far the commonest periphrasis for God is in fact heaven. Matthew is the most Jewish of the Gospel writers; Mark was not so strictly Jewish; and Luke was a Gentile, who was not bound at all by the Jewish conventions and customs. So it comes about that Matthew with his strong orthodox Jewish background prefers to speak of *the kingdom of heaven,* while Mark and Luke, being less affected by Jewish tradition, have no hesitation in speaking of *the kingdom of God.*

If we wish to define the kingdom of God, we may best find the basis of our definition in the Lord's Prayer. The outstanding characteristic of Jewish literary style is parallelism. The Jew tended to say everything twice;

and the second form of expression is a repetition, an amplification, or an explanation of the first. Almost any verse of the Psalms will demonstrate this characteristic. Almost all the verses of the Psalms have a division in the middle, and the second half of the verse repeats or amplifies the first half.

God is our refuge and our strength,
A very present help in trouble (Psalm 46. 1).

The Lord of hosts is with us;
The God of Jacob is our refuge (Psalm 46. 7).

He maketh me to lie down in green pastures;
He leadeth me beside the still waters (Psalm 23. 2).

In the Lord's Prayer two phrases occur side by side (Matthew 6. 10):

Thy kingdom come,
Thy will be done in earth as it is in heaven.

Let us, then, apply the principle of parallelism to these two phrases, and let us assume that the second explains and interprets the first. We then arrive at the definition: The kingdom of God is a society upon earth in which God's will is as perfectly done as it is in heaven.

Quite clearly this personalises the kingdom of God, for such a society cannot begin to exist until each individual man and woman perfectly accepts the will of God. That is to say, whenever anyone fully accepts the will of God, that person is within the kingdom of God. No man can be a citizen of any country, unless he is willing to accept the laws of that country; citizenship and obedience to a country's laws go hand in hand. Exactly in the same way, no man can be a citizen of the kingdom of God, until he fully accepts the laws of God. To be a citizen of the kingdom of God, to be in the kingdom of God, to possess the kingdom of God, all mean perfectly to accept the will of God.

If that be so, this Beatitude is saying: O the bliss of the man who has realized his own utter helplessness and his own utter inadequacy, and who has put his whole trust in God; for then he will humbly accept the will of God, and in so doing he will become a citizen of the kingdom of God. And that is precisely the origin of the bliss, for in doing his will is our peace.

CHAPTER IV

THE BLISS OF THE BROKEN-HEARTED

Blessed are they that mourn, for they shall be comforted (MATTHEW 5. 4).

Of all the paradoxes of the Beatitudes surely this is the most violent. It is an astonishing thing to speak of the joy of sorrow, of the gladness of grief, and of the bliss of the broken-hearted. The word which the Authorised Version translates *mourn* (*penthein*) is one of the strongest words for mourning in the Greek language. It is used for mourning for the dead. Very often it is associated with the word *klaiein*, which means *to weep*, and it signifies the sorrow which issues in tears.

From the very word which is used to describe this mourning two things are immediately clear. It is the sorrow which pierces the heart; it is no gentle, sentimental, twilight sadness, in which a man can languish and luxuriate; it is a sorrow which is poignant, piercing and intense. It is the sorrow which is visible; it is the sorrow which can be seen in a man's bearing, a man's face, and a man's tears. It is the sorrow which a man is bound to show to the world and to show to God, because he cannot help doing so. What, then, did Jesus mean, when He spoke of the bliss of the broken-hearted?

i. It may well be that, at least to some extent, this Beatitude is meant to be taken quite literally. There is no doubt that sorrow has a value of its own, and that it has a place in life which nothing else can take. There is always something missing in life, until sorrow has entered into life. There is an Arab proverb which says: "All sunshine makes a desert." It is told that once Elgar, the great musician, was listening to a young girl singing. She had a beautiful voice and a well-nigh faultless technique, but she just missed greatness. "She will be great," said Elgar, "when something happens to break her heart." There are things which only sorrow can teach.

It might well be said that sorrow is the source of the great discoveries in life. It is in sorrow that a man discovers the things which matter, and the things which do not matter. It is in sorrow that a man discovers the meaning of friendship and the meaning of love. It is in sorrow that a man discovers whether his faith is a merely superficial ornament of life or the essential foundation on which his whole life depends. It is in sorrow that a man discovers God. "When you come to the bottom," said Neville Talbot, "you find God."

There is a deep sense in which it is literally true that sorrow has its own unique blessedness to give.

ii. Luke repeats this Beatitude in a slightly different form: "Blessed are ye that weep now, for ye shall laugh " (Luke 6. 21). It would seem that Luke was thinking in terms of the necessary struggle of the Christian life, and that he meant that, if a man accepts the cross which is at the heart of the Christian life, then quite certainly he will win the crown.

Luke had firmly grasped the truth that in this life and from this life a man gets what he chooses. If he chooses to live as if nothing mattered beyond this world, then he gets all that this world has to offer. But, if he chooses to live in the conviction that there is something far more important beyond this world, then in this world he may meet all kinds of trouble, and by this world's standards he may be a failure, but there awaits him a joy which this world cannot give. In the Dives and the Lazarus parable there is a picture of Dives in hell, asking mercy from Abraham. But Abraham said to him: "Son, remember that thou in thy lifetime receivedst thy good things, and likewise Lazarus evil things: but now he is comforted and thou art tormented" (Luke 16. 25).

In life two choices are always confronting a man. Will he take the course of action which will provide an immediate profit, an immediate happiness, and an immediate freedom from trouble? Or, will he take the course of action which necessitates immediate discipline, and which will provide immediate trouble, and which may mean present hardship and present persecution and present sacrifice? The Christian teaching is clear. It is the man who is prepared to accept the present toil and the present tears who will know the ultimate and permanent bliss.

iii. It may be that this Beatitude at least to some extent means that blessedness belongs to those who sorrow for the sin, the sadness and the suffering of this world. It may describe the man whose heart is touched for those who are in the midst of what Virgil called

" the tears of things ", whose sense of justice is challenged by those who are suffering from tyranny and oppression and injustice, to whom the appeal of weakness and suffering and pain never comes unheard.

It is always right, according to the Christian point of view, that a man should be detached from *things;* but it is never right that he should be detached from *people*. It was Jesus' teaching in the Parable of the Sheep and the Goats (Matthew 25. 31-46) that a man's attitude to him is seen in that man's attitude to other people. In many ways the most unchristian of all sins is the sin of contempt. In *The Patrician* John Galsworthy makes Miltoun say: " The mob! How I loathe it! I hate its mean stupidities, I hate the sound of its voice, and the look on its face—it's so ugly, it's so little!" George Bernard Shaw once said: "I have never had any feeling for the working classes, except a desire to abolish them, and to replace them by sensible people." Carlyle, thinking of the political unwisdom of the country, once said: " There are twenty-seven and a half million people in this country—mostly fools."

That is the precise opposite of the teaching of Jesus, and of the attitude of Jesus. Repeatedly it is said of Jesus in the Gospels that he was *moved with compassion* Mark 1. 41; 6. 34; 8. 2). The word is *splagchnizesthai,* which is the strongest word for compassion in the Greek language. *Splagchna* are the *bowels,* and *splagchnizesthai* means to be moved to the very depths of one's being. The basic meaning of the Incarnation is that God cared so intensely for men that in Jesus Christ he deliberately chose to identify himself with the sin, the sorrowing and the suffering of the human situation. Those whose names are written in gold letters in the honour roll of humanity are not those who looked at their fellow-men with a conscious and a contemptuous superiority, nor are they those who regarded the struggles of mankind with a cool detachment; they are those who cared so much, and who sorrowed so much, that the sorrow of their hearts drove them to spend their lives in the service of mankind. The world would be an infinitely poorer place without those who sorrowed dynamically for their fellow-men.

iv. We have not even yet come to the full depth of the meaning of this Beatitude. The real meaning of it is: "Blessed is the man who is moved to bitter sorrow at the realization of his own sin." The way to God is the way of the broken heart. Penitence is the first act of the Christian life, and penitence is sorrow. Paul said: "Godly sorrow worketh repentance to salvation" (II Corinthians 7. 10). Long before Paul, the Psalmist had said: "I will declare mine iniquity; I will be sorry for my sin" (Psalm 38. 18). The beginning of the Christian life is the utter dissatisfaction with life as it is. Augustine, telling of the days before his conversion says: "I grew more wretched, and Thou didst grow nearer."

In the spiritual biography of Paul there is a strange progression. It is likely that Galatians is the first letter which Paul ever wrote, and that he wrote it about the year A.D.48. In the first sentence of it he calls himself "Paul an apostle" (Galatians 1. 1). Without hesitation he lays claim to the highest office in the Church; it is on

29

his possession of that office he bases his claim to write. Seven years later in the year A.D.55 he was writing to the Corinthians. There he writes: " I am the least of the apostles, and not fit to be called an apostle " (I Corinthians 15. 9). By that time he had come to think of the office of an apostle as something to which he had little right and little claim. Another eight years went by and about A.D.63 he wrote the letter called the Letter of the Ephesians, and in it he says: " Unto me who am less than the least of the saints is grace given " (Ephesians 3. 8). In the New Testament *saint* is the word for *church member* (cp. Ephesians 1. 1; Philippians 1. 1). By that time Paul had begun to think of himself, not as an apostle, but as barely fit to be a member of the Church at all. At the very end of the day, when he was awaiting death, he wrote to Timothy, and in that letter he writes: " Christ Jesus came into the world to save sinners of whom I am chief " (I Timothy 1. 15). Here the man whom all the world regarded as the supreme servant of Jesus Christ calls himself the chief of sinners. Nor is there any cause for surprise in all this.

The longer a man knows Jesus Christ, and the nearer he comes to Jesus Christ, the more two things are bound to enter into his life. First, he is bound to see more and more clearly that standard of perfection in Christ by which he must judge his own life. A man may think he does a thing well—until some day he sees a real expert doing it; and then he knows how inadequate his own standard of performance is. A man may think that he is a fairly satisfactory person, and that he has nothing to worry about—so long as he compares himself with his neighbours and with his fellow-men; but the question that the Christian has to ask is not, "Am I as good as my neighbour?" but, "Am I as good as Jesus Christ?" No human being can ever have any cause for satisfaction when the standard against which he sets himself is Jesus Christ. Such a comparison leaves him in constant mourning that he falls so far short. Second, the more a man knows Jesus Christ, the more he realizes the cost of sin. If the effect of sin was to necessitate the death on the Cross of the loveliest life which was ever lived, then sin stands revealed in all its terribleness, and a man knows that he can do nothing but mourn so long as sin has one last vestige of a place within his life.

Penitence is an attitude of mind to which a man must be reawakened every day, and, therefore, the godly sorrow of repentance is always a blessed thing, for it is the gateway to the joy of forgiveness.

But this Beatitude does not leave the matter there. To leave the matter there might well leave a man so weighted down with a sense of sin that he would be driven to despair. This Beatitude goes on to make its promise: "Blessed are they that mourn, *for they shall be comforted*." There is more in this promise than any single word can ever translate. The word which is translated *comforted* is the passive of the verb *parakalein,* which is a word with a wealth of meaning.

i. *Parakalein* does mean *to comfort* or to *console,* but it may be worth while remembering that that in fact is the rarest of all its meanings, and is not found in classical Greek at all. But beyond a doubt comfort is part of the meaning of the word here. The man who goes to God with godly sorrow for his sin will receive the comfort of God. There is a wide variety of reactions with which a penitent sinner may be received. If he goes to the one whom he has wronged to confess his sin, he may be received with adamantine implacability and turned sternly away; he may be received with a grudging concession of forgiveness which falls far short of the restoration of fellowship which true forgiveness involves; he may be received with a kind of forgiveness, a forgiveness which agrees to forgive, but which never consents to forget. There are all kinds of limitations in human forgiveness. But when a man goes to God in godly sorrow for his sin, he receives the full welcome of the love of God, and in that love his sorrow is abundantly comforted.

ii. But *parakalein* has more meanings than that. It is the word which is used for to summon to one's side as an ally, a helper, a counsellor, a witness, and it is the word which is used for to invite to a banquet. Here, then, is something more. God does not only accept and receive the sinner back again. He treats him, not as a criminal, but as an honoured guest. He does not treat him as if he could never trust him again; he invites him to become his ally, his helper, his witness among men. In the magnificence of his grace God sends us back to the field of our defeat in the certainty that his grace can turn our past defeat into future victory.

iii. *Parakalein* has a still further series of great implications. It means *to exhort* or *to encourage*. Aeschylus, for instance, uses it for troops cheering each other as they enter into battle (*Persae* 380). Aristotle uses it of stimulating and energising the mind (*Nicomachean Ethics* 1175. 7). It is used of inciting and exciting a person, and of fomenting a fire until it bursts into a flame (Xenophon, *Cyropaedia* 7. 5. 23.).

Here, then, is the greatness of the forgiveness of God. When a man goes to God with the godly sorrow of repentance, he is not comforted only with the joy of past sins forgiven and forgotten; his heart is filled with courage; his mind is stimulated to new thought and new understanding and new adventure; the flickering flame of his life is fanned to a flame. His whole life is caught up into the strength and the beauty of God.

Blessed are they that mourn for they shall be comforted. There is blessedness in sorrow; there is blessedness in taking the right way even when the right way is the hard way; there is blessedness in sorrow for the sins and the sorrows and the sufferings of men; there is supreme blessedness in the godly sorrow which leads to that repentance which receives the forgiveness of God. And when that forgiveness comes, there is comfort for the remorse of the heart, there is the glory of being trusted on the field of our defeat, there is the encouragement, the stimulus, the flame in life which God alone can give.

CHAPTER V

THE BLISS OF THE DISCIPLINED SELF

Blessed are the meek, for they shall inherit the earth (MATTHEW 5. 5).

The real greatness of this Beatitude is hidden from modern eyes, because the word *meek* has come down in the world. To modern ears it describes a weak, flabby, milk and water, spineless creature, lacking in all virility, submissive and subservient to a fault, unable to stand up for himself or for anyone else. But that is very far from the original meaning of the word. The meaning of the word is, in fact, so great and so comprehensive that it defies translation.

The word is *praus,* and it has a double ancestry, and its two ancestries look in different directions. One of them looks to God and one of them looks to men. One of them has to do mainly with a man's attitude to God; the other has to do mainly with a man's attitude to his fellow-men.

The first ancestry of the word is its Hebrew ancestry. *Praus* is the word which is used to translate the Hebrew word *anaw*. In the Authorised Version *anaw* is translated *humble, lowly* and *meek*. It is a favourite word in the Psalms, and it describes the man, who in loving and obedient humility accepts the guidance of God and the

34

providence of God, and who never grows resentful and bitter about anything which life may bring to him, in the certainty that God's way is always best, and that God is always working all things together for good. In the Psalms such a man is very dear to God, and stands in a very special relationship to God. God hears the desire of the *humble,* and never forgets their cry (Psalm 9. 12; 10. 17; 34. 2; 69. 32). God scorns the scorners but gives grace to the *lowly;* it is better to be of a humble spirit with the lowly than to divide the spoil with the proud (Proverbs 3. 34; 16. 19). The *meek* shall eat and be satisfied (Psalm 22. 26). God guides the *meek* in justice, and teaches them his way (Psalm 25. 9). God rises in judgment to save the *meek* of the earth; he lifts up the *meek* but casts down the wicked; he pleads the cause of the *meek;* he beautifies the *meek* with salvation; the *meek* shall increase their joy in the Lord (Psalm 25. 9; 76. 9; 147. 6; 149. 4; Isaiah 11. 4; 29. 19). It may well be that arrogant men will oppress the *meek* (Amos 2. 7); but it is God's promise that the *meek* will inherit the earth (Psalm 37. 11).

In Hebrew thought the man who is *meek, anaw,* is the man who obediently accepts God's guidance, who humbly accepts whatever God sends, and who is, therefore, dear to God, and whose life is strengthened and beautified by the gifts which God can give only to such a man.

When we turn to the Greek ancestry of the word *praus,* we find an equal wealth of meaning.

We begin by noting a simple, but very significant, use of the word *praus.* It is used, as is the corresponding

Latin word *mitis,* to describe an animal which has been tamed and domesticated and which has become subject to control. It is, for instance, used of a horse which has been broken in and which has become obedient to the reins, and of a sheep-dog who has been trained by kindness to understand and to obey every word of command. Even from this we can see that *praus* describes that which is *under control.*

It is Aristotle who deals at length and repeatedly with the quality of *praotes,* and with the man who can be called *praus.* It was Aristotle's practice to describe every virtue as the mean between two extremes. On the one hand there was an extreme of excess; on the other there was an extreme of defect; and in between there is the virtue itself. So on the one hand there is *recklessness;* on the other hand there is *cowardice;* and between them there is the mean which is *courage.* So, then, Aristotle says that *praotes* is "the observance of the mean in relation to anger" (*Nicomachean Ethics* 4. 5. 1). It is the mean, the correct and happy medium, between excessive anger and excessive angerlessness. On the one hand there is the man who is mean and small spirited; on the other hand there is the man who is irascible, passionate, bitter, and harsh-tempered; and in between there is the man who is *praus.* The man who is *praus* "feels anger on the right grounds, against the right persons, in the right manner, at the right moment, and for the right length of time." Such an attitude of mind becomes angry "only in such a manner, for such causes, and for such a length of time as principle may ordain" (*Nicomachean Ethics* 4. 5. 3). In the *Eudemian*

Ethics (3. 3. 4) the man who is *praus* is defined as "neither too hasty- nor too slow-tempered. He does not become angry with those he ought not to, nor fail to become angry with whom he ought." The little tract on *Virtues and Vices* (4. 3) says: "To *praotes* belongs the ability to bear reproaches and slights with moderation, and not to embark on revenge quickly, and not to be easily provoked to anger, but to be free from bitterness and contentiousness, having tranquillity and stability in the spirit."

To all this we must add two other facts about the Greek view of this virtue of *praotes*.

It is the virtue of the man who acts with gentleness, when he has it in his power to act with stern severity. So it is used of a king who might have exercised vengeance on a rebellious people but who treated them with kindliness. It is used of a ruler who might have dispensed strict justice, but who dispensed forgiveness. It is used of a commander who might have dealt with an erring subordinate with unsparing discipline, but who used a sympathetic leniency. The man who is *praus* is the man who, as Browning said, knows well that it is good to have a giant's strength, but it is tyrannous to use it like a giant.

In Greek thought the virtue of *praotes* is again and again associated with *strength*. *Praotes* is not the gentleness which has its source in weakness, or in indifference, or in fear, or in a slack and unprincipled tolerance. It is the gentleness of strength. So when men spoke of Cyrus, as Xenophon tells us, "one spoke of his wisdom, another of his strength, another of his *gentleness* (*praotes*), and another of his beauty and of his commanding presence." In Plato the character of the guardian of the state is sketched. Such a man must treat his friends with *gentleness* and his foes with sternness. He must be *gentle* and spirited. He must have the passion which will right wrong and challenge injustice, but he must have the *gentleness*, which will see in the wrong-doer a sick man to be healed, and an erring mortal to be restored to the right way. So, then, *praus* signifies strength and gentleness combined.

Praus, meek, has in it an attitude to God and an attitude to men.

In its Godward look it describes the man who gives to God the perfect trust, the perfect obedience, and the perfect submission. It is the attitude of Job when he said: "The Lord gave, and the Lord hath taken away; blessed be the name of the Lord" (Job 1. 21). "Though he slay me yet will I trust him" (Job 13. 15). It is the attitude of Mary, the mother of Jesus, when she said: "Behold the handmaid of the Lord; be it unto me according to thy word" (Luke 1. 38). It is the attitude of Paul, when, all resistance broken, he said: "Lord, what wilt thou have me do?" (Acts 9. 6). It is the attitude of the hymn-writer, when he said:

> My times are in thy hand:
> Why should I doubt or fear?
> My Father's hand will never cause
> His child a needless tear.

It is the attitude of Jesus when he said: "Not as I will, but as thou wilt. Thy will be done" (Matthew 26. 39, 42). It is the attitude of the man who in every

38

age finds what Aristotle called "tranquillity and stability" in committing himself into the hands of God.

In its manward look this Beatitude in effect says: "Blessed is the man who is always angry at the right time and who is never angry at the wrong time." "Be angry and sin not," said Paul (Ephesians 4. 26). Anger is one of God's greatest gifts to men. But anger is like a strong medicine, which if it is used in the right way, can do infinite good, and which, if it is used in the wrong way, can do infinite harm. What, then, is the rule for anger? When anger is for our own sake, it is always wrong. When anger is for the sake of others, it is often divinely right. When we look at Jesus, we never see him angry at the slights, the insults, the injuries which he himself received. But we see his eyes glint with anger, as he looked round on the coldly orthodox Scribes and Pharisees who placed the observance of the details of the Sabbath law above the healing of a man with a withered hand (Mark 3. 5). We see his eyes blaze with anger when he saw the money-changers and the sellers of doves making an iniquitous profit out of the poor pilgrims in the Temple Court, for it was there that the Christ of love became the Christ of the whip (Matthew 21. 12; Mark 11. 15; Luke 19. 45; John 2. 14, 15).

To be right anger must be selfless anger. It must be an anger which is not destructive but saving, not lacerating but healing. The world would be a poorer place without the power of righteous anger, and it is precisely that anger that the man who is *meek, praus,* possesses in his heart.

Every word to be fully understood must become flesh;

every great virtue and quality to be fully demonstrated must be incarnated in a person. It is so with this quality of meekness. In the Bible the quality of meekness is connected specially with two people. It was said of Moses that he was very *meek*, above all men which were on the face of the earth (Numbers 12. 3). It was Jesus' claim for himself: "I am *meek* and lowly in heart" (Matthew 11. 29). History has never seen a leader with more strength and force of character than Moses, nor a leader with a greater gift of righteous anger, when there was occasion for it. The world has never seen more dynamic power than the power which throbbed in the personality of the man Jesus of Nazareth. That is the meekness which is blessed.

To the meek a promise is made, and the promise is that " they will inherit the earth." This Beatitude is a direct quotation of Psalm 37. 11, so it will be to the Old Testament that we must first go in order to interpret its meaning.

The word *inherit* has in the Bible a different meaning from the meaning in which we commonly use it. We commonly use the word to mean to enter into possession of something which has been left in a will; but in the Bible the word usually means to enter into possession of something which has been promised and foretold by God. Further, it will help us to see the original meaning of this phrase, if we remember that it can be equally well translated: "The meek shall inherit *the land*." This promise has three stages in it.

i. Originally it had to do with the entering of the children of Israel into the promised land. God had promised Abraham that he would give him the promised land to inherit it (Genesis 15. 7). It was God's promise that he would give to the Jews the land of Palestine as an inheritance (Deuteronomy 4. 38). So, originally this was a promise that if the children of Israel were obedient to God, if they committed their ways to him to trust him and to obey him, then one day they would enter into the land which he had promised them, and that they would dwell there in prosperity and peace. The great truth behind this is that obedience and trust are the conditions of entering into possession of the promises of God. Any man who chooses to go his own way will arrive in the far country and not in the promised land.

ii. As time went on, the Jews came to see that by human means they could never become great; their nation was too small and the world was too great. So they began to look for the coming of the Messiah, the entry of God's Anointed King into the world, the coming of one who would lead them into all the bliss and the blessing of the Messianic age. So the promise of the Psalmist came to mean something greater than the possession of the land of Palestine; it came to mean that the meek, those who humbly trusted God and who obediently accepted his will, would enter into all the blessings of the Kingdom of God upon earth. It is those who spend their lives waiting upon God who will be ready for the Kingdom when it comes.

iii. But with the coming of Jesus Christ this Beatitude acquires a new width and a new greatness. For us it means far more than the possession of any territory upon earth; for us it does not mean that we have to wait for

41

bliss and blessedness until the coming of the Messianic Age in some distant future beyond the hills of time. It means the promise of life here and now; and that promised life has two things in it.

It has *peace*. The man who has committed himself and all his ways to God has a peace that the world cannot give nor ever take away, for he knows that nothing can pluck him from the hand of God, and that no experience of life can separate him from the love of God.

It has *power*. Meekness means the mastery of anger and passion. The man who is *praus* is the man who has such self-mastery that he is always angry at the right time and never angry at the wrong time. "He that is slow to anger is better than the mighty; and he that ruleth his spirit than he that taketh a city" (Proverbs 16. 32). Self-discipline is the way to strength; self-mastery is the way to power; and he who rules himself is indeed a king among men. To have the discipline of meekness is to have the power which makes life great, for only when a man has mastered himself is he able to rule others.

And now we can take the Greek aspect of *praus* and the Hebrew aspect of *praus* and put them together. From the Hebrew point of view the man who is *praus* is committed to God in perfect obedience and in perfect trust; from the Greek point of view the man who is *praus* is the man who has every instinct and every passion under discipline and under control. Therefore, in the final analysis, the man who in peace and in power inherits life, is not the man who is *self-controlled,* for such self-control is not in man's power as all experience shows, but the man who is *God-controlled*. And so the

42

final meaning of this Beatitude is: " O the bliss of the man who has so committed himself to God that he is entirely God-controlled, for such a man will be right with God and will be right with self and will be right with men, and will enter into that life which God has promised and which God alone can give."

CHAPTER VI

THE BLISS OF THE STARVING SOUL

Blessed are they which do hunger and thirst after righteousness, for they shall be filled (MATTHEW 5. 6).

It takes far more than a dictionary to define the meaning of a word, especially when a word is a word of human experience. When a word is a word of experience, then the experience of him who uses it, and of those who hear it, will define its meaning. Clearly the word *pain* means something quite different to a person who has never had a day's illness in his life, and to a person who has passed through a furnace of physical agony. Clearly the word *love* will mean something quite different to a child of ten, a youth or a maiden of twenty, a mature adult of middle age, an aged one who is far down the vale of years. Words which describe an experience have a basic meaning, but it is life which decides what the intensity of that meaning is.

It is so with the Beatitude which tells of the bliss of the starving soul. This saying would mean something quite different to a Palestinian audience in the time of Jesus from that which it means to a twentieth-century audience which enjoys all the plenty which social and economic development have brought. There are few in our situation who have ever known what it is to be genuinely hungry. In Palestine in the time of Jesus the wage of a working-man was eightpence a day. No one ever grew fat on that; and, if for the day labourer there was even one day's unemployment, then actual hunger invaded the home. Eric F. F. Bishop in *Apostles of Palestine* tells us that even in the twentieth century one of the Commissions despatched to Palestine during the time of the Mandate estimated the average income of a peasant family at £24 a year. For a family to eat meat was in Palestine a rare experience. In that ancient world hunger was not something which could be satisfied with a passing snack. It could often be the hunger which threatened life, the starvation in which a man had to eat or die. The same is true of thirst. There are few in our situation who have ever known what it is to be genuinely thirsty. We live in a situation in which we turn a tap and water flows. In that ancient world men were dependent on streams and wells, and there might be a long, long distance between them on a journey, and the water-skin might be empty. Still worse, the sand-storm might come, and all that a man could do was to turn his back to the swirling sand, and hide his head in his hood, while his mouth and his throat and his nostrils and his lungs were filled with the fine sand, which made him choke with thirst. People who lived in conditions like that knew the thirst which has to be satisfied, if a man is to survive. What Jesus is saying here is: " Blessed is the man who longs for righteousness as a starving man longs for food, and as a man perishing of thirst longs for water."

This is a metaphor which the psalmists and the prophets used to describe the longing of the soul for God. As the hart pants for the water brooks, so the soul of the psalmist thirsts for the living God (Psalm 42. 1, 2). The soul of the psalmist thirsts for God, as in a dry parched land where there is no water (Psalm 63. 1). The invitation of the prophet is that he who thirsts should come and take of the water of life freely (Isaiah 55. 1). Here is a picture of a time when water had to be *bought*. In *Eastern Customs in Bible Lands* H. B. Tristram tells of sitting in the Eastern bazaars, with little or no shelter from the pitiless sun and hearing "the sonorous and ceaseless cry of the water-bearer as he perambulates the narrow streets," and seeing the way-farers buying water at a *para* a drink.

Here, then, Jesus is confronting his disciples with a promise which is also a challenge and a demand. What he meant by *righteousness* we shall later have to investigate, but he is saying here: "Do you desire righteousness with that intensity of desire with which a starving man desires food, and a man parched with thirst desires water?" This is a challenge and demand with which Jesus continually confronted men. It was with this challenge that he confronted the Rich Young Ruler (Matthew 19. 16-22; Mark 10. 17-22; Luke 18. 18-23). The young man came to Jesus pleading to be enabled to find eternal life, real life. He was an attractive character for, when Jesus looked at him, he loved him. In answer to Jesus' questions he claimed that he had kept all the commandments from his youth upwards. Jesus then confronted him with the demand that he

46

should go and sell all that he had and give the proceeds to the poor. In effect Jesus was saying to him: "Do you want eternal life as much as that? Are you prepared to sacrifice the luxuries of this life to gain eternal life?" And, when the matter was put that way, the young man went sorrowfully away. It was with this challenge that Jesus confronted one of the men who wished to follow him. The man said that he would follow Jesus anywhere. Jesus answered: "Foxes have holes, and birds of the air have nests; but the Son of Man hath not where to lay his head" (Luke 9. 57, 58). In effect Jesus said to that man: "Do you want to follow me enough to face a life like that?" It was with this challenge that Jesus confronted his disciples when he told them that they must love him more than father or mother or any other of their kith and kin (Matthew 10. 37; Luke 14. 26). In effect he said to them: "Do you want to become my disciple enough to give me the unconditional first place in your life?" In view of all this this Beatitude has four things to say about the Christian life.

i. It uncompromisingly lays down the demand of the Christian life. This is the most demanding of the Beatitudes; it insists that the Christian life is not for the dilettante; it is not even for the interested and the attracted; it is for those who desire righteousness as a matter of life and death. In the novel *Quo Vadis?* there is a picture of a young Roman called Vinicius. He is in love with a Christian girl, but because he is a pagan she will not return his love. Without her knowledge he followed her to the little secret gathering of the Christians, and there he heard Peter preach. As he listened something happened within him. He knew that Jesus Christ was the most important reality in life, but, " He felt that, if he wished to follow that teaching, he would have to place on a burning pile all his thoughts, habits and character, his whole nature up to that moment, burn them into ashes, and then fill himself with a life altogether different, and an entirely new soul." That is the demand of Christianity. The Christian does not say: " I am interested in Christ." He says: " For me to live is Christ " (Philippians 1. 21). He does not say: " I would like to come to terms and to some arrangement with this Jesus." He says: " I surrender to Jesus Christ."

ii. By implication it lays down the main cause of failure in the Christian life. That cause of failure is simply that we do not sufficiently desire to be a Christian. It is the experience of life that, if a man desires a thing sufficiently, he will get it. If he is prepared to bend every energy, to sacrifice everything, to toil with sufficient intensity, to wait with sufficient patience, he will succeed in getting that on which he has set his heart. The great barrier to our becoming fully Christian is our failure to desire it enough, our deep-rooted unwillingness to pay the price of it, our fundamental desire not to upset life, but to keep it as it is. Luke gives us a different, and a complementary, version of this Beatitude: " Woe unto you that are full! for ye shall hunger " (Luke 6. 25). That means: " Woe unto you who are satisfied, who are content with things as they are, who have no passionate desire for that which you have not got. You may live

48

comfortably enough just now, but the day comes when you will discover that you have somehow missed the greatest things of all." In *The Master of Ballantrae* Robert Louis Stevenson describes how the master left the ancestral home at Durrisdeer for the last time. He had not been a good man, but in that moment he was sad. He turned to his steward McKellar. "Ah, McKellar," he said, "do you think I have never a regret?" "I do not think," said McKellar, "that you could be so bad a man unless you had all the machinery to be a good one." "Not all," said the master, "it is there you are in error—the malady of not wanting." The biggest barrier to the full entry into the Christian life is nothing other than the malady of not wanting— and that is what this Beatitude lays down.

iii. We have already said that this is the most demanding of all the Beatitudes; but it is also the kindest and most encouraging of the Beatitudes. It is the Beatitude which tells us of the sympathy of God for the struggler on the Christian way. It is not he who has *attained* righteousness, who is called blessed, but he who *hungers and thirsts for it*. If the blessedness was for those who had achieved, it would be for none; but it is not for those who achieve in this case, it is for those who long. The mystery of man is not the sin of man; the mystery of man is the goodness of man. In man there is an instinctive love of goodness, and an instinctive power to recognise it. It is easy to cite on the other hand the great evil men of history, the men who seem to have been born without any moral sense, without pity and without compassion; but, if we take the ordinary run of men, there is in man an instinctive recognition of, and desire for, goodness.

In his autobiography H. G. Wells drew a contrast between "the secret splendour of our intentions," and the poverty of our achievements. "A man may be a bad musician," he says, "and yet be passionately in love with music." Thomas à Kempis said: "Man sees the deed, but God sees the intention." And that applies in both directions. God does not see only the mixed and impure motive that may lurk behind that which looks like a good deed; he also sees the longing for goodness and the love of goodness which lies behind the sins and the mistakes of life. Sir Norman Birkett, as he then was, the great lawyer and judge, looking back on the many criminals he had met once said: "They are condemned to some nobility; all their lives long the desire for good is at their heels, the implacable hunter." Robert Louis Stevenson spoke of those who had made shipwreck of life "clutching the remnants of virtue in the brothel or on the scaffold". When David wished to build a house unto God, it was not given to him to do so—that was reserved for his son Solomon—but nevertheless God said to him: "Thou didst well that it was in thine heart" (I Kings 8. 18). This Beatitude blesses not only the deed, but also the dream that never came true.

iv. It may well be that this Beatitude tells us of the totality of Christian goodness. It is quite true that in later Greek, such as the Greek of the New Testament, the grammatical niceties of the classical period break down; but there is in this Beatitude a grammatical point which may well be of the greatest importance. In classical Greek

50

verbs of hungering and thirsting normally take the genitive case after them; the genitive case is the case which we express by the word *of*. In the phrase, " a slice of bread ", *of bread* is the genitive case. The reason for this grammatical usage is that normally we hunger and thirst for part of some supply of food or drink. We do not want the whole loaf; we want a part *of the loaf*. We do not want the whole pitcher; we want some *of the water* which is in the pitcher. But, when these verbs do take the direct accusative, it means that the person involved wants *all* the food and *all* the drink there is. If a Greek said, " I hunger for bread," or, " I thirst for water," and the words *bread* and *water* were in the accusative case, it would mean that he wanted the whole loaf, and the entire contents of the pitcher. In this Beatitude *righteousness* is in the accusative case; and, therefore, if we are to translate this with strict accuracy, we ought to translate it: " Blessed are those who hunger and thirst for *all of righteousness,* for total righteousness."

That is what so seldom happens. There are people against whose moral character no possible fault can be found; they are completely respectable; intemperance, gambling, adultery, swearing, dishonesty, failure to pay their debts could never possibly be attributed to them; but they are cold and hard and without sympathy. No one who had made a mistake could lay his head on their shoulder, and sob out his sorry story. They are good, but they are cold. On the other hand there are people who have all kinds of faults; they may drink to excess; their language may at times be lurid; their

51

passions are not always under control; it is easy to point at their moral errors and their failure in the respectable virtues. But, if anyone else is in trouble, they would give him the coat off their back, and hand him their last penny without a thought of grudging it. Their morals may be erratic, but their heart is warm. The truth is that in neither of these cases can you say that these people are *good* in the full sense of the term. Each of them has a *part* of goodness, but not the *whole* of it; each has *fragmentary*, but not *total* goodness. The Christian goodness is a complete goodness in which virtue and love join hands.

We have not yet sought to define what this word *righteousness* means. The word is *dikaiosune*, and it has three meanings which are all possible, and all relevant. It means *justice;* it means *righteousness* in the sense of right-living; and it is the word which is used for the *justification* which comes by faith. Let us look at it in each of these three senses.

i. *Blessed are those who hunger and thirst for justice.* This burning desire for justice may move in two directions. (a) There are those who urgently and intensely desire justice for themselves, and for the cause for which they stand. There are those who are conscious of their own rectitude, conscious of their own complete commitment to Jesus Christ, and for whom life has been an agonising thing, but who yet refuse to believe that that is the end of the story. In the Revelation the souls of the martyrs cry out to God, asking how long it will be before he vindicates them (Revelation 6. 10). Such a desire for justice, such a confidence in the justice and in the honour of God, such a refusal to be driven to despair by the events of time, is the demonstration of complete trust in the power and will of God to vindicate in time or in eternity those who entrusted all things to him. This is the spirit of the man who can say: "I know whom I have believed, and am persuaded that he is able to keep that which I have committed unto him against that day" (II Timothy 1. 12). "I believe," said Robert Louis Stevenson, "in an ultimate decency of things, and, if I woke up in hell, I would still believe in it."

(b) There are those who urgently and intensely desire justice, not so much for themselves, as for those who are suffering from injustice. This has been the motive of all the great social reformers. J. E. McFadyen entitled the book of Amos "A Cry for Social Justice". Amos is appalled and enraged by the robbery and violence which have their homes in great houses, and by those who take bribes and refuse justice to the poor (Amos 3. 10, 12). His anger is hot against those who swallow up the needy, those who give short measure, and who overcharge even for that, in their lust for profit, those who accept the very bodies of the poor in payment of their debts (Amos 8. 4-6). There are those who have had such a hunger and thirst for justice that they could never be content in a civilization in which the law is weighted in favour of one colour or one class; in a society in which the few have too much and the many too little; in an economic system in which men are treated, not as persons, but as things.

It is true that those who intensely desire justice that

God's cause may be vindicated, and who urgently seek for justice for those to whom life is unjust, are blessed.

ii. *Blessed are those who hunger and thirst for righteousness.* In Greek ethics *dikaiosune* was a great word; it is the virtue of the man who is constantly observant of his duty to the gods and his duty to men. In Greek the man who is *dikaios* is the man who pays what he owes to the gods and to men. In this sense righteousness is that love of God, which issues in complete trust and absolute obedience; and that love of men, which issues in selfless service and unwearied forgiveness.

Blessed indeed is the man whose most passionate desire is to love God and to love men as he ought.

iii. *Blessed are those who hunger and thirst for justification.* In Paul *dikaiosune* is what we know as justification by faith. The Greek verb which is translated *to justify* is *dikaioun.* It does not mean to find reasons why a man is right, as it does in English. It does not even mean to make a man just. It means to treat and to accept a man as a just and a good man. When God justifies the sinner, God in his mercy and grace accepts the sinner as if he was a good man. Clearly this at once introduces a new relationship between God and man. So long as we think of God as the stern and inexorable judge and law-giver, there can be nothing between us and God but distance, estrangement and fear. But once we know that God is ready to accept us and to love us and to forgive us just as we are, the distance is replaced my intimacy, the estrangement by friendship, the fear by loving and grateful trust. This is justification by faith; and, therefore, the basic and essential meaning of justification is *a right relationship with God*. To be justified is to be in a right relationship with God; and justification is such a relationship. So, then, if we take this meaning this Beatitude will mean; "Blessed is the man whose most intense desire is to enter into a right relationship with God."

It is not necessary that we should choose between these meanings. We may well believe that this Beatitude includes all these things, and that the hunger and thirst of which it speaks are for the vindication of the cause of God and for justice for all men; for that personal righteousness which loves and obeys God and serves and forgives men; for that right relationship with God in which all the fear and the estrangement have turned into confidence and trust. No man could hunger and thirst for any greater gifts than these.

After the affirmation there comes the promise. "Blessed are they that hunger and thirst after righteousness; *for they shall be filled.*" The word which is used for *filled* is an extraordinary word. It is the word *chortazesthai*. Originally this word was used to describe the special fattening of animals for killing. When it did come to be used of men, it meant to stuff a person full to the point of complete satiety. It always remained something of a colloquial word, and it always retained something of the idea of filling a person full to repletion. If a man hungers and thirsts for that righteousness which God alone can give, God will not send him empty away, but God will fill him, until his longings are achieved and his soul is satisfied.

CHAPTER VII

THE BLISS OF THE KIND HEART

Blessed are the merciful, for they shall obtain mercy
(MATTHEW 5. 7).

This Beatitude has to be set against two backgrounds;
it has to be set against the background of the Old
Testament, and it has to be set against the background of
the contemporary world in which it was spoken.

Mercy, *chesedh*, is one of the great words of the Old
Testament. In the Old Testament it occurs more than one
hundred and fifty times, and on more than nine-tenths of
the occasions when it does occur the reference is to
God and to the action of God. Great as the word mercy
is, it may be that the use of this word mercy to translate
chesedh has done something to narrow and to belittle its
meaning. For the most part we think of mercy in terms
of the remission of penalty, or the relaxing of a demand
which might have been enforced. In ordinary usage, to
have mercy upon a man is to agree not to treat him with
the sternness and the severity and the rigorous justice
which he deserves. But *chesedh* is a far more positive
thing than that. *Chesedh* is translated *mercy* ninety-six
times in the Authorised Version, but it is also translated
kindness no fewer than thirty-eight times, and it is
kindness which is the basic idea of the word. *Chesedh,*

when it is used of God, is the outgoing kindness of the heart of God. It is the basis of God's whole relationship to man, and especially of his relationship to his people Israel.

It is to God that mercy belongs (Isaiah 62. 12), and it is in mercy that God delights (Micah 7. 18). The mercy of God is so infinite that it reaches the heavens (Psalm 36. 5; 57. 10), and it is so enduring that it lasts for ever (Psalm 89. 1, 2; 100. 5; 103. 17). One of the most often repeated of all statements in the Old Testament is that the mercy of God endureth for ever (I Chronicles 16. 34; II Chronicles 7. 3; Ezra 3. 11; Psalm 106. 1; 107. 1 138. 8; twenty-six times in Psalm 136; Jeremiah 33. 11).

This mercy of God is demonstrated in the events of history. It is to be seen in the deliverance from Egypt (Exodus 15. 13), and in the kindness of the Persian king, when he allowed the exiles to return to Jerusalem (Ezra 9. 9).

Not only is God's mercy demonstrated in the events of history, it is to be seen in nature and in the very structure of the world. The earth is full of the mercy of God (Psalm 119. 64), and it is in the mercy of God that the rain and the sunshine come (Job 37. 13).

Wherever a man looks, to the events of history or to the processes of nature, he is confronted with the outgoing mercy of God. It is this mercy which decides all man's relationships with God. It is the ground of man's appeal to God in the time of trouble. " Save me," cries the Psalmist, " for thy mercy's sake " (Psalm 6. 4; 31. 16; 49. 26). It is the ground of man's appeal for forgiveness when he knows that he has sinned and disobeyed God. It is to the fact that God is long-suffering and of great mercy that Moses appeals for forgiveness for the perversity of the people (Numbers 14. 18, 19). The Psalmist lifts up his soul to God, because God is plenteous in mercy (Psalm 86. 5). It is the ground of the trust and the serenity of the good man. The Psalmist has trusted in God's mercy (Psalm 13. 5; 52. 8), and he knows that through the mercy of God he will not be moved (Psalm 21. 7). It is the mercy of God which gives a good man hope (Psalm 33. 18; 57. 3; 59. 10; 90. 14). It is the mercy of God which gives him joy, even in the day of his trouble (Psalm 31. 7). It is the ground of the assurance with which the good man meets life. From heaven God sends his mercy and his truth to save (Psalm 57. 3; 61. 7). It is the ground of the gratitude of the good man to God. The Psalmist sings of God's mercy, for God has been his defence in the time of trouble (Psalm 59. 16). It is through the mercy of God that prayer is heard (Psalm 66. 20). That mercy of God can and does deliver even from death and the grave (Psalm 86. 13). That mercy is the source of the good man's strength, for it is it which upheld him when his foot slipped (Psalm 94. 18).

When we examine the occurrences of the word mercy in the Old Testament we find that it is connected with what the Authorised Version calls *truth* oftener than with anything else. God did not leave Abraham destitute of his mercy and his truth (Genesis 24. 27). The paths of the Lord, as the Psalmist has found, are mercy and truth (Psalm 25. 10; 36. 5; 57. 3; 61. 7; 89. 14; 98. 3; 115. 1). The word for *truth* is *emeth;* and it does not mean intellectual truth; it means *steadfastness* and complete *fidelity* to a promise. So, then, the mercy and the truth of God go together. The outgoing love of God is no capricious thing, changing, as it were, with the mood of God; it is something on which men can absolutely depend because it is founded on the fidelity and the steadfastness of God to himself and to his promises.

That is why again and again the mercy of God is connected with the lives of the great characters in the Old Testament story. It was in the mercy of God that Lot escaped from Sodom (Genesis 19. 19). Jacob sees his life directed and kept by the mercy of God (Genesis 32. 10). It was the mercy of God which directed Joseph's amazing rise to success when he was sold as a slave boy into Egypt (Genesis 39. 21). It is the mercy of God which is with David the king, and which gives him a son to succeed him (II Samuel 7. 15; 22. 51; I Kings 3. 6). It is the mercy of God which has directed the history of Israel (Psalm 106. 7). In every case these men who made history would have said with the hymn-writer:

With mercy and with judgment
My web of time He wove.

We have now seen that this *chesedh,* this mercy, is specially connected with the fidelity and the steadfastness of God, and with God's direction of the lives of his servants and his people. Here we come to the basic and the essential characteristic of the relationship of which *chesedh* is the expression. In more than twelve places in the Old Testament the word *mercy* is connected with the word *covenant.* God is the faithful God who keeps *covenant and mercy* with those who love him (Deuteronomy 7. 9). The Psalmist hears God say of his Anointed King: "My mercy will I keep for him for evermore, and my covenant shall stand fast with him" (Psalm 89. 28). The ideas of *mercy* and *covenant* are inseparably connected. The idea of the covenant is basic to the whole Old Testament. The covenant means that God graciously entered into a special relationship with the people of Israel, a relationship in which he would be their God and they would be his people, a relationship which was initiated by God alone, but which is to be maintained by the obedience of the people to the Law which God had given them (Exodus 24. 1-8). In that covenant relationship *chesedh* is God's attitude to his beloved people. *Chesedh* is God's steadfast and faithful adherence to his special relationship to his own people; it is the outgoing love of God to his people within that special relationship into which he entered with them, and to which he will never be false. That is why Sir George Adam Smith very beautifully translated *chesedh* "leal love". *Chesedh* is the loyal outgoing love of God to his own people.

It is exactly in this relationship that we have the explanation of another aspect of this mercy. It is, of course, true in one sense to say that outgoing love of God goes out to all men; but at the same time it is also true that in another sense there are certain conditions to be fulfilled. The condition of the covenant was that the people should obey and serve the Law of God. The Law was read to them and the people said: "All that the Lord hath said will we do, and be obedient" (Exodus 24. 7). Therefore, again and again in the Old Testament we find that this mercy is specially to those who love God and who keep his commandments (Exodus 20. 6; Deuteronomy 5. 10; 7. 9). It it to those who walk before the Lord with their whole heart (I Kings 8. 23). It is to such as keep his commandments and his testimonies (Psalm 25. 10). It is towards them that fear him (Psalm 103. 11), and to them that devise good (Proverbs 14. 22). God's loyalty is doubly rich in its gifts to those who are loyal to him.

Since this *chesedh,* this mercy, is the characteristic of God in his relationship with men, it is only to be expected that God wishes this mercy to be the characteristic of men's relationships with each other, and there is always condemnation for the man who fails to reproduce it in his life. It is the complaint and condemnation of the Psalmist that the wicked remembered not to show mercy (Psalm 109. 16). The warning of the wise man is, " Let not mercy and truth forsake thee " (Proverbs 3. 3). It is the charge of Hosea that there is no truth, nor mercy, nor knowledge of God in the land (Hosea 4. 1). He warns men to observe mercy and justice (Hosea 12. 6), and he warns them that nothing, not even sacrifice, can take the place of mercy in the sight of God (Hosea 6. 6). Micah sums up the whole duty of man in the commandments to do justice, to love mercy, and to walk humbly before God (Micah 6. 8), and Zechariah appeals for justice, mercy and love toward our brother (Zechariah 7. 9).

In the Old Testament mercy is no negative thing; it is not merely the agreement to suspend judgment, to remit penalty, to mitigate justifiable and deserved severity. It is the outgoing love of God to his covenant people, a love to which God is pledged and to which he will be for ever true, a love which is seen in the processes of nature and in the events of history, a love on which the whole relationship of man and God depend, an outgoing love which men must reproduce in their relationships with each other.

In the Greek of the New Testament the Hebrew *chesedh* becomes *eleos*. The word is not so common in the New Testament; it occurs twenty-seven times. But the use of it is highly significant.

God is rich in mercy (Ephesians 2. 4), and it is that mercy which saved us (Titus 3. 5). It is that mercy which we find at the throne of grace (Hebrews 4. 16); it is that mercy which gives us hope through the Resurrection of Jesus Christ (I Peter 1. 3), and through which Jesus Christ confers eternal life upon us (Jude 21). A particularly significant usage of it is that Paul connects the mercy of God with the giving of the gospel to the Gentiles (Romans 9. 23; 11. 31; 15. 9). The outgoing love of God has gone even further out and has embraced, not only the people of the original covenant, but all mankind.

We do not find the word often on the lips of Jesus, but the importance he attached to it is clear. Twice Jesus quotes the saying of Hosea, that God wants mercy and not sacrifice (Hosea 6. 6; Matthew 9. 13; 12. 27). His condemnation of the Pharisees is that they have been meticulous about the details of the ceremonial law, and have forgotten the great essentials—justice, mercy and faith (Matthew 23. 23). The Parable of the Good

Samaritan is mercy in action, and all are bidden to go and to imitate that mercy (Luke 10. 37). It is clear that Jesus too saw this outgoing love as the great characteristic of the relationships of the Christian with his fellow-men.

We must now set this Beatitude against its second background, against the background of the pagan world in which it was first spoken. A Christless world is a callous world, and mercy was never a characteristic of pagan life. Sir Henry Holland, the famous medical missionary from Quetta, whose work on eye troubles is world famous, tells how sometimes a patient would be brought in, in whom the trouble was so far advanced that his eyes were beyond the help of surgery. When he had to break news like that to a patient, the by-standers would roar with laughter, and tell the patient to begone and not to be a nuisance to the doctor. Sympathy was unknown. One of Mary Slessor's most heart-breaking problems in Calabar was the fact that the Africans dreaded twins, as being of evil omen. They were never allowed to live; they were killed, crushed into an earthenware pot, and flung to the leopards to devour. A world without Christ is a world without mercy. Let us look at certain of the merciless elements in the world of New Testament times.

The Jew was merciless to the sinner and merciless to the Gentile. As Jesus saw it, there is joy in heaven over one sinner who repents (Luke 15. 7, 10); as the Jewish teachers saw it, " There is joy before God when those who provoke him perish from the world." Jesus believed in salvation; the Jews believed in obliteration. It is true that some Jewish teachers held that the poor of the

Gentiles must be helped, their sick visited, and their dead buried equally with Jews; but that was not orthodox belief. According to the Law it was forbidden to help a Gentile mother and her child even in the crisis of childbirth. If a Jew had become a renegade from the faith, it was not even lawful to summon medical attention for him, even if his life was in danger. The Gentiles were to be killed as snakes are crushed; they were created for no other purpose than to be fuel for the fires of Hell. There is little mercy there.

In the Roman world life was merciless especially to the slave and to the child. The slave, as Aristotle said (*Nicomachean Ethics* 8. 11. 6) was no different from a living tool, and what consideration can a tool receive? A master could, and did, kill his slave, as when Vedius Pollio flung his slave to the savage lampreys in the fishpool of his courtyard, because he had stumbled and broken a goblet (Pliny, *Natural History* 9. 23). It is Cato's advice when he writes on agriculture: "When you take possession of a farm, look over the livestock and hold a sale. Sell your oil, if the price is satisfactory, and sell the surplus of your wine and grain. Sell worn-out oxen, blemished cattle and sheep, wool, hides, an old wagon, old tools, an old slave, a sickly slave, and whatever else is superfluous" (*On Agriculture* 2. 7). Juvenal tells of the haughty mistress being dressed by her slave-girl for an appointment. "Why is this curl standing up?" she asks, and then down comes a thong of bull's hide to inflict chastisement for the offending ringlet (*Satires* 6. 486-492). There are masters who "delight in the sound of a cruel flogging, thinking it sweeter than the sirens' song", who are never happy "until they have summoned a torturer and can brand someone with a red hot iron for stealing a couple of towels", who "revel in clanking chains" (Juvenal, *Satires* 14. 16-22). Of course there were kindly masters, but officially, so to speak, there was no such thing as sympathy for a slave, who was not even a human being.

The ancient world practised the exposure of children. The unwanted child was simply thrown out like refuse. Hilarion writes to his wife Alis in 1 B.C. with the strangest mixture of love and callousness:

Hilarion to his wife Alis, warmest greetings. . . . I want you to know that we are still in Alexandria. Don't worry if, when they all go home, I stay on in Alexandria. I beg and entreat you, take care of the little child; and, as soon as we get our pay, I will send it up to you. If—good luck to you!—you bear a child, if it is a boy, let it live; if it is a girl, throw it out. You told Aphrodisias to tell me, "Don't forget me." How can I possibly forget you. Don't worry.

The exposure of an unwanted child was normal routine. In Stobaeus (*Eclogues* 75) there is a saying: "The poor man raises his sons, but the daughters, if one is poor, we expose."

An exposed child might be picked up and trained for the brothels, or, worse, it might be deliberately maimed, and then used by some professional beggar to awaken the sympathy and extract the alms of the passers-by.

The child who was weak or sickly or ill-formed had little chance of survival. In the *Republic* (460 B) Plato insists that only the children of better unions must be kept, and any defective child must be done away with. "Let there be a law," says Aristotle, "that no deformed child shall be reared" (*Politics* 7. 14. 10). Even Seneca lays it down: "Mad dogs we knock on the head; the fierce and savage ox we slay; sickly sheep we put to the knife to keep them from infecting the flock; unnatural progeny we destroy; we drown even children who at birth are weakly and abnormal. It is not anger but reason which separates the harmful from the sound" (*On Anger*, 1. 15. 2). The sheer callousness of the pagan world is almost inconceivable to a world which has known Christian mercy.

As a last example of the failure of mercy in the pagan world, we take the text on which all the great Greek tragic dramas were written—"The doer shall suffer." It was the Greek conviction that from the moment a man did a wrong thing Nemesis was on his heels, and would not rest until the man was destroyed. It was the Greek conviction that the whole universe was designed to smash the sinner. A God of mercy was beyond their ken.

Here, then, is the background against which Jesus spoke of the bliss of the merciful. What did he mean by this mercy which the Christian is to show in his life and in his relationships with his fellow-men? The essence of the whole matter is that the merciful are those who bear towards others that outgoing love which reflects and reproduces the outgoing love of God. To be merciful is to have the same attitude to men as God has, to think of men as God thinks of them, to feel for men as God feels for them, to act towards men as God acts towards them. Clement of Alexandria once made the startling statement that the true Christian Gnostic "practises being God"; and that is exactly what being merciful means. Let us, then, more closely define this mercy.

First and foremost, this mercy is *outgoing* love. If it is outgoing, it is necessarily first *outlooking*. Mercy is the reverse of self-centredness; it is something which the man who concentrates on himself can never possess in his heart and can never show in his life. It is the antithesis of selfishness. It is the attitude of the man for whom the needs of others are more clamant than his own, and the sorrows of others more poignant than his own. This mercy is not possible so long as a man consciously or unconsciously regards himself as the centre of the universe. As Nels Ferré has said in *Christ and the Christian*: "The Church is the fellowship of the dead-to-themselves and the alive-for-Christ." Mercy comes when love of self is replaced by love of God and love of man, which are the fulfilment of both the great commandment of Jesus Christ and of the life of Jesus Christ.

This mercy is necessarily an *individualised* outgoing love. It is not a vague generalised benevolence. A sentimental love of humanity can often go hand in hand with a complete failure in personal relationships and a failure to love the fellow-men with whom we daily and actually come into contact. The outgoing love of the Christian is an outgoing love, not of humanity, but of men. The great and precious characteristic of Jesus is that again and again we find him giving all of himself to each individual person. It is quite possible to profess and even to feel a large benevolence for mankind, and at

67

the same time to find the claims of some individual man nothing more than a nuisance. This outgoing mercy is a mercy which in fact goes out to my neighbour, as well as to mankind.

This could well be expressed by saying that this mercy is *actualised* outgoing love. It is not simply a sentiment; it is a life. It is not simply an emotion; it is action. The New Testament does not say: "God so loved the world", and stop there; it says, "God so loved the world that he gave his only begotten Son" (John 3. 16). This mercy is an outgoing love for man which actualises itself in action for individual men. Florence Allshorn said: "An ideal is not yours until it comes out of your finger-tips." This mercy lodges in the heart, but expresses itself in the hand. The desire to help becomes the deed of help, as it did in the case of God.

It remains to ask what this mercy, this *chesedh,* this outgoing love is. Love is a word with so many shades of meaning that we must try to define it more closely. T. H. Robinson says of *chesedh*: "It means a sympathetic appreciation of other persons; the power, not merely to concentrate blindly upon them, but to feel deliberately with them, to see life from their point of view." That is to say, *chesedh,* mercy, means the ability to get right into the other person's skin until we can see with his eyes, think with his mind, and feel with his heart. And that is to say that *chesedh,* mercy, comes from self-identification with other people. And herein lies the problem of mercy; most people are so concerned with their own thoughts and feelings and selves that they seldom or never even think of making this deliberate attempt to identify themselves with the mind and heart and life of their fellow-men. Mercy is far more than a wave of emotional pity; it is even more than help, as we think help to be needful. It comes from the willingness to forget self, and to make the deliberate and conscious effort to identify ourselves with other people. If we could and would make that self-identification with other people, certain great consequences would immediately follow.

It would make *tolerance* much easier. There is always a reason why a person thinks as he does think, and by entering into that person's mind and heart, and by seeing things with his eyes we could understand that reason, and tolerance would be much easier. John Wheatley was one of the famous Clyde-side members of Parliament. He spoke like a fire-brand and a revolutionary, and was regarded as a rebel. He was once talking to King George the Fifth. The king asked him why he was so violent an agitator. Wheatley quite simply told the king something of the slums of which he knew so much, and of the life that people had to live there, and of the spectre of unemployment, and the life of the working-man. When he had finished, the king said quietly: "If I had seen what you have seen, I too would be a revolutionary." The king had seen the world with Wheatley's eyes, and understood. Tolerance is only possible when we make the effort of self-identification with others.

It would make *forgiveness* much easier. There is always a reason why a person acts as he does. To know all is so often to be able to forgive all. It is easy to condemn a person or an action, when we are judging from the outside. No man has any real right to condemn another man until he has stood in the same position, and faced the same temptation, and come through the same battle. We cannot literally do that, but we can make the effort to identify ourselves with the other person, and when we do so there will come the understanding which leads to forgiveness.

It would make any *help* we give much more effective. There is a way of giving which we would never use, if we identified ourselves with the person to whom the help is given, for there is a way of giving which can do nothing but hurt and humiliate. On very many occasions our giving is decided by what we wish to give, or by what we think is good for the other person, and such giving may well not be the help that the other person stands in need of. If we made the effort of self-identification with others, then we would know both how to give and what to give.

So, then, this mercy, this *chesedh,* this outgoing love depends on a deliberate self-identification with our fellow-men. We have already seen that this mercy is a reflection and a reproduction in our attitude to our fellow-men of the attitude of God to all men. We, therefore, reach the final truth about this mercy. The supreme demonstration of this mercy is the Incarnation. In Jesus Christ God literally entered into our skin, seeing things with our eyes, thinking things with our minds, feeling things with our hearts. The Incarnation is God's complete self-identification with the sins, the sorrowings, and the sufferings of men. The supreme example of mercy is God's identification with men in Jesus Christ. The outgoing love of God was such that he made this supreme and sacrificial self-identification with man; and that is why God understands, forgives, and saves.

The Beatitude ends with the promise: "Blessed are the merciful, for they shall obtain mercy." Here is an inescapable principle laid down by Jesus. "With what judgment ye judge, ye shall be judged; and with what measure ye mete, it shall be measured to you again" (Matthew 7. 2). "If you forgive men their trespasses, your heavenly Father will also forgive you; but if ye forgive not men their tresspasses, neither will your Father forgive your trespasses" (Matthew 6. 14, 15). "He shall have judgment without mercy that hath showed no mercy" (James 2. 13). As a man judges, so he will be judged; as a man acted towards his fellow-men, so will God act upon him. It could not be otherwise. If this mercy, this outgoing love, this self-identification with others is the characteristic of the nature of God, then he who has practised it in his life will become more and more like God; and he who has made no attempt to practise it in his life will become ever and ever more distant from God. The practice of mercy is that which unites us with God; the failure in mercy is that which separates us from God. And so the ending of this Beatitude is promise and warning at one and the same time.

CHAPTER VIII

THE BLISS OF THE PURE
IN HEART

Blessed are the pure in heart, for they shall see God
(MATTHEW 5. 8).

In this Beatitude, the Greek word that is used for *pure*
is a word with a very great width of meaning. It is for
that reason all the more necessary to study its meaning,
and to define the sense in which the Beatitude uses it.

The word is *katharos*. In classical and in secular Greek
it begins with a purely physical meaning, and can be used
of clothes which are clean in contrast with clothes which
are soiled and dirty. It has a whole series of meanings
which have to do with things which are without blemish,
without admixture, and without alloy. It is used of pure
water, and of wine and milk which are not adulterated
by water; of animals which are physically perfect, and
have no blemish; of grain which is winnowed from all
chaff, and of white bread which is made of the best of
flour; of silver and gold which have no alloy in them, but
which are sterling in their quality; of an army which has
been cleansed of all disaffected and inefficient soldiers
and which is a first-class fighting force, purged of every
undesirable element. It is used of blood, lineage, descent
which are absolutely pure, and of language which is

pure of all colloquialisms, errors of grammar and infelicities of style. It is used of a man who has been cleared of debt and who has been granted an absolute discharge from some duty which he has now fulfilled. It is used of a man who is ceremonially pure, and who is ceremonially fit to enter into the temple of his god. And, finally, it enters fully into the moral world and means free from pollution, free from defilement, and free from guilt. Very often it is used in epitaphs to pay tribute to one who all his or her life kept virtue unsullied and untarnished. The kindred word *katharsis* means *a purging draught,* which cleanses the body of all impurities. Here we clearly have a word with a very great history and a very wide variety of meanings.

But, as always when we wish to find the meaning of a word in the New Testament, we must look at the meaning of the word *katharos* in the Old Testament. In the Greek Old Testament *katharos* is very common, and occurs more than one hundred and fifty times. When we examine its use we find that it has two definite and distinct meanings. In the great majority of cases it describes *ceremonial* purity, the kind of foods and animals which may be eaten, the purity which comes from ceremonial washings and from all the observance of ritual laws, the kind of purity which is a matter of the observance of rules and regulations and which has little or no moral content at all. In Exodus *katharos* occurs thirty-seven times and in Leviticus it occurs thirty-four times and in no instance does it ever describe anything but this ceremonial and ritual purity. But *katharos* does, although not nearly so frequently, describe moral and

73

spiritual purity. It is used of Abraham in the sense of integrity (Genesis 20. 5, 6), although the action of which it is used was a very doubtful action. It is used to describe blamelessness in face of a charge of misconduct (Genesis 44. 10). In Job it is used in the sense of innocent, upright, clear in the sight of God, and to describe the prayer of a good man (Job 4. 7; 8. 6; 11. 4; 16. 17). In the Psalms it is used of the pure heart and of the clean heart (Psalm 24. 4; 51. 10). Isaiah uses it to mean clean and pure from sin (Isaiah 1. 16). And it is the word which is used in Habakkuk (1. 13) when it is said of God that he is of purer eyes than to behold iniquity.

From all this one thing emerges quite clearly. In the ancient world there were two conceptions of purity. One conception regarded purity as a matter of ritual observances, as the continual obedience to a set of conventional regulations and taboos, as entirely a ceremonial matter. The other conception regarded purity as a matter of life and conduct and a state of mind and heart.

First of all, let us look at the purity of ritual observance. The very fact that *katharos* is so often used in this sense in the Greek Old Testament is the proof of how common and deep-seated and widespread this idea of purity was. There were certain animals which were clean and certain which were unclean (Leviticus 11). To touch a dead body rendered a man unclean for seven days (Numbers 19. 11-13). Before an orthodox Jew sat at meat he washed his hands in a certain way, not in the interests of hygiene, but in the interests of this ritual and ceremonial purity. First of all he had to hold each hand with the fingers pointing upwards, and pour

74

water over the hands until it reached at least up to the wrist; then he had to cleanse each palm by rubbing it with the fist of the other hand; then he had to hold the hands with the fingers pointing downwards, and pour water from the wrist so that it ran down the hand and off by the fingers. Not to do so was to be unclean, impure. On the Day of Atonement the High Priest had to wash his whole body in clean water five times, and his hands and feet ten times. Meticulously to observe these conventional rituals and ceremonies was held to make a man pure and to render him well-pleasing to God.

Another aspect of this comes out in the regulations governing elegibility for the priesthood. To be a priest a man must be a descendant of Aaron. Moral quality, spiritual insight, goodness, virtue, piety, holiness did not enter into the matter. With certain physical provisos, which we shall go on to see, if a man was a descendant of Aaron nothing could stop him being a priest; and if a man was not a descendant of Aaron all the saintliness and all the goodness in the world could not make him a priest. A man might be an arrogant sinner, an adulterer, an exploiter of his fellow-men; if he was a descendant of Aaron, he was a priest. A man might live with the grace of God irradiating him; if he was not a descendant of Aaron, he could not be a priest. The one proviso which limited this was the fact that the Law laid down one hundred and forty-two physical blemishes which disqualified a man from serving as a priest at the sacrifices in the Temple. Any physical blemish however small ruled a man out.

From this point of view purity had been completely

externalised; it was a matter of observing certain rituals and ceremonies; and the heart did not enter into it at all. So long as a man went through the conventional observances, he was pure.

That was what we might call the official and orthodox conception of purity in the time of Jesus; and Jesus completely contradicted it and dissociated himself from it in two words—Blessed are the pure *in heart*.

For Jesus purity was an inward thing, a thing of the heart and of the mind and of the attitude of the soul. On the orthodox Jewish point of view a man might have within his heart thoughts of arrogance and pride, thoughts of bitterness and hate, unclean thoughts and desires, but, so long as he observed the outward rituals correctly, he was pure. On Jesus' point of view, even if a man's outward actions were impeccably correct, and even if he observed every detail of the ceremonial law with meticulous devotion, he might still be utterly impure, because the thoughts of his heart were not right.

We need not be too quick to condemn the orthodox Jewish idea of purity as fantastically and obviously wrong. It is still possible to identify religion with outward observances. It is still possible to regard a man as a religious man because he observes all the outward conventions of religion—Church-going, Christian liberality, Bible-reading, respectability, pious language and the like—while in the eyes of Christ that man is utterly irreligious because the thoughts of his mind and the desires of his heart will not bear the scrutiny of God.

What, then, was this purity which Jesus demanded? It

is not surprising that by many this purity has been identified with sexual purity; but that is to narrow the meaning far too much. Origen (*Homily 73, on John*) says that it means "not only those who have been rid of fornication, but those who have been rid of all sins, for every sin leaves a stain upon the soul". We must go much deeper than that, for in his outward actions a man might strictly observe sexual purity and yet in his inmost thoughts transgress daily against it.

If we go back and re-examine the meanings of *katharos*, when it is used apart from ceremonial purity, we shall see that nearly all the other meanings of the word have one common element; they all describe something which has no tainting admixture of anything else. Unmixed milk or wine, unalloyed silver, winnowed corn are all *katharos*. They have no element in them to affect their purity. We can, therefore, say that "Blessed are the pure in heart" means "Blessed are those whose thoughts and motives are absolutely unmixed, and, therefore, absolutely pure." This Beatitude describes the bliss of the heart whose thoughts, motives, desires are completely unmixed, genuine, sincere.

When we realize what this Beatitude is saying it is the most demanding of all the Beatitudes. It necessitates the strictest and the most honest self-examination, and the end of that self-examination will infallibly be humiliation. Even an action which looks absolutely generous and even sacrificial may have in it some residue of self-satisfaction, of self-display, and of pride, even when we are scarcely conscious that it is so. In even the finest things there may be a lurking taint of pleasing self and courting the approval of men, even when we do not know it, until we rigorously search our own hearts. Even a man who to others seems a saint may, when he examines himself, find that he is the chief of sinners. There is no way to the purity that this Beatitude demands other than the death of self and the springing to life of Christ within the heart. Only the Christ who spoke this Beatitude can enable any man to enter into the bliss which this Beatitude promises.

The promise of this Beatitude is that the man who is pure in heart will see God. Even within the promise there is a warning. The very fact that the vision of God is promised to the pure in heart necessarily means that there are those to whom that vision cannot be given. It is a fact of life that what we see depends not only on what is in front of our eyes but also on what is within our minds and hearts. Knowledge makes a difference to seeing. The man who knows nothing of botany will see by the wayside a tangle of weeds and grasses and wild-flowers to none of which he can put a name; the skilled botanist will call each by name, and maybe will see something rare and unusual. The man with no knowledge will go out into the night and see in the sky above him a mass of lights. He will not be able to name one of them, and will not be able to tell a star from a planet. The skilled astronomer will walk amongst the stars, calling them by name like his familiar friends; and by these same stars, which mean nothing to the man without knowledge, the navigator will bring back his ship to harbour. A doctor can tell things by looking at a patient as a layman never can; a scholar can see truth and beauty in a manuscript which is unintelligible to the man with no knowledge. What we know determines what we see. Experience makes a difference in seeing. That which leaves us quite unmoved when we are young, that which may even amuse a child, brings a stab to the heart and tears to the eyes, when the years have interpreted it and given it meaning. Moral character and the state of a man's mind make a difference to what he sees. A man can have a mind so depraved and unclean that he can see something to snigger about in anything, while to the pure all things are pure. It is so with us and God. Each day in life we are either fitting or unfitting ourselves to see God; we are either coming nearer to him or drifting further from him; we are making ourselves either more and more open or more and more shut to the vision of himself which he desires to send us.

The idea of seeing God is something which would immediately strike an answering chord in the heart and mind of people of the day of Jesus. The greatest privilege that a servant or a courtier could have was to have the right constantly to stand in the presence of the king, constantly to see his face, and to hear his wisdom. When the Queen of Sheba had heard all the wisdom of Solomon, she said: "Happy are thy men, happy these thy servants, who stand continually before thee, and hear thy wisdom" (I Kings 10. 8). The inmost group of the king's counsellors and friends were called "men of the king's presence" (II Kings 25. 19).

Even so, it was the great desire of men to see God as a king's friend saw their king. "I beseech thee," said

Moses, "shew me thy glory" (Exodus 33. 18). The greatest bliss that the Psalmist can imagine is to behold God's face in righteousness, and to be satisfied, when he awakes, with the likeness of God (Psalm 17. 15). It is his hope that because of his integrity God sets him before his face for ever (Psalm 41. 12). His great desire is to see the power and the glory of God as in the past he has seen them in the sanctuary of God (Psalm 63. 2). The upright will dwell in the presence of God (Psalm 140. 13). Bliss is to be for ever in the presence of God.

There are times when in Scripture it is said that it is impossible for any man to see God. It is God's answer to Moses: "There shall no man see me and live" (Exodus 33. 20). When Manoah discovered who his heavenly visitor had been, he said in terror to his wife: "We shall surely die because we have seen God". (Judges 13. 22). But to see God is not literally to see God with the physical eye; that is not possible. "No man hath seen God at any time" (John 1. 18). To see God means two things.

It means to enter into fullness of knowledge of God. It is what Paul meant when he said: "Now we see through a glass, darkly; but then face to face: now I know in part; but then shall I know even as also I am known" (I Corinthians 13. 12). It means to have done with guessing and groping and to see and to know the truth.

It means to enter into the intimate fellowship of love. Love's highest joy is to be in the presence of the loved one. Mrs. A. R. Cousin wrote the lines, paraphrasing the thoughts of Samuel Rutherford:

I shall sleep sound in Jesus,
 Fill'd with His likeness rise,
To live and to adore Him,
 To see Him with these eyes.

. . . .

The Bride eyes not her garment,
 But her dear Bridegroom's face;
I will not gaze at glory,
 But on my King of grace—
Not at the crown He gifteth,
 But on His nail-pierced hand;
The *Lamb* is all the glory
 Of Immanuel's land.

The man whose heart has been cleansed in Jesus
and by the Spirit of God, the man whose motives,
thoughts, emotions, desires are absolutely unmixed, will
be given nothing less than the vision of God. The
beginning of the fulfilment of this promise will be even
here in time, but the completing of it will need all
eternity. Even here we have in Jesus Christ a new and
living way into the presence of God, but hereafter the
rending veil will reveal to us God as he is, if we
have kept ourselves pure in his grace, and the search for
knowledge will find its answer, and the desire of love
will find its satisfaction in the presence of God.

CHAPTER IX

THE BLISS OF THE BREAKER-DOWN OF BARRIERS

Blessed are the peacemakers, for they shall be called the children of God (MATTHEW 5. 9).

It may well be that time's changes in the meaning of words have narrowed for us the meaning of this Beatitude. For us peace is largely a negative word; it tends to describe mainly the absence or the cessation of war and trouble. Even in a situation in which a land was devastated, in which cities were in ruins, and in which men, women and children were starving, if war came to an end, we would likely say that peace had returned. But for a Jew peace had a far wider meaning than that. The Greek word for peace is *eirene,* which translates the Hebrew word *shalom. Shalom* has two main meanings. It describes perfect welfare, serenity, prosperity and happiness. The eastern greeting is *Salaam,* and that greeting does not only wish a man freedom from trouble; it wishes him everything which makes for his contentment and his good. For the Jew peace is a condition of perfect and complete positive wellbeing. Second, *shalom* describes right personal relationships; it describes intimacy, fellowship, uninterrupted goodwill between man and man. It can easily be seen that peace does not describe only the absence of war and strife; peace describes happiness and well-being of life, and perfection of human relationships. When the Psalmist prays that peace should be within the walls of Jerusalem (Psalm 122. 7, 8), he is praying that every good blessing should descend upon the city and upon its citizens.

It would be true to say that the New Testament is the book of this peace. In it the word *peace, eirene,* occurs eighty-eight times, and it occurs in every book. One of the great characteristics of the New Testament letters is that they begin and end with a prayer for peace for those who are to read and to listen to them. Paul begins every one of his letters with the prayer that grace and peace may be on the people to whom he writes, and often the New Testament letters end with some such phrase as, "Peace be to you all." When Jesus was leaving his disciples, as John tells the story, he said to them: "Peace I leave with you, my peace I give unto you" (John 14. 27). J. S. Stewart has called that the last will and testament of Jesus. Of worldly goods and possessions Jesus had nothing to leave, but he left to men his peace.

We must mark one all-important fact in this Beatitude —the people to whom the blessing is promised. The people who are blessed are not the peace-*lovers* but the peace-*makers*. It can happen that a man is a peaceful man and a peace-lover, and is yet not a peace-maker. A man may know that there is something wrong in some situation, in his family, in his Church, in some group of which he is a member; he may know that something ought to be done to rectify the situation; but he may also know that any step taken to mend the situation may well involve difficulty and trouble and problems which it will not be pleasant to face. In such a situation a man may well decide to do and say nothing, as he will put it, "for peace's sake". He will allow the situation to continue and the whole matter to drift uneasily on, because his love of a certain kind of peace makes him evade all trouble. Such a man may be called a peaceable man and a peace-lover; but he is certainly not a peace-maker; he is rather in the end a trouble-maker; for the longer any situation is allowed to continue the more serious its consequences and the harder its cure. The man who is blessed is the man who is prepared to face difficulty, unpleasantness, unpopularity, trouble in order to *make* peace. The peace of which this Beatitude speaks is not the spurious peace which comes from evading the issue; it is the peace which comes from facing the issue, and from being prepared to give everything in toil and in sacrifice which the situation demands. In his translation Luther translates the Greek by the word "peaceable", but in the margin he adds and explains this by saying that it means "those who make and preserve peace among one another; and they are more than peaceable."

Let us then look at the meaning of this peace whose makers are blessed.

Peace, *shalom,* as we have seen, means welfare and well-being at their best and at their highest. Therefore, this Beatitude means that all those who do anything to increase the well-being and the welfare of the world are blessed. The work of social reformation is work for God. Those whose zeal and toil produce houses

84

which are fit to live in and conditions which are fit to work in are in the realest sense servants of God. Those who find new ways of conquering pain and healing the sick, those who toil that the hungry may be fed and that the aged may be tended are in the realest sense doing the work of God. Those who do anything to make life in the world fuller and happier and easier for others are truly serving God. If all men are the children of God, then their heavenly Father cares how they live, how they work, how they are fed and clothed, how they are treated in weakness, in want, in age and in pain. The man with a passion for the welfare of his fellow-men is serving God in serving men, and is therefore blessed.

We get even nearer to the meaning of this Beatitude when we take peace, *shalom,* in its other meaning of *right relationships.* The Jewish Rabbis taught that those who honour father and mother, those who do good, and those who make peace between people reap good fruits alike in this life and the life to come. In every man's life there are three relationships; and in each case it is of the greatest importance that the relationship should be right.

There is a man's *relationship to himself,* and blessed, indeed, is the man who has succeeded in coming to a right relationship with himself. This is the sense in which the early fathers of the Church frequently took this Beatitude. Clement of Alexandria took it to be a blessing on " those who have stilled the incredible battle which goes on in their own souls ". Augustine took it to be a blessing on those " who have composed and subjected to reason all the motions of their minds, and who have tamed their carnal desires ".

85

It is a fact of experience that every man is at least to some extent a split personality. It was the Jewish belief that in every man there were two natures, the good nature which drew him up, and the evil nature which dragged him down. It was as if a good angel stood at his right hand beckoning him to goodness, and an evil angel stood at his left hand beckoning him to evil. Life has been described as "an endless war of contrarieties". This is the struggle of which Paul wrote so movingly in the seventh chapter of Romans. "The good that I would, I do not; but the evil which I would not, I do" (Romans 7. 19). There was a war in his members between two laws, the one urging him to goodness, the other enticing him to sin. This was the picture which Plato drew of human nature. He pictured the soul as a charioteer. Yoked to the chariot there are two horses. The one horse is wild and untamed; the other is gentle and under control. The name of the first horse is passion, and the name of the second horse is reason; and somehow the soul has to control them and to make them run in double harness. A. E. Housman in one of his verses vividly expresses the universal human experience:

> More than I, if truth were told,
>> Have stood and sweated hot and cold,
> While through their veins, like ice and fire,
>> Fear contended with desire.

Robert Burns was well aware of the wreckage which he so often made of life. "My life," he said, "reminded me of a ruined temple; what strength, what proportion in some parts, what unsightly gaps, what ruin in others."

Studdert Kennedy describes the feelings of a soldier in the first world war. The public tried to treat him as a hero; the padre insisted on treating him as a hell-deserving sinner.

> Our padre says I'm a sinner,
> And John Bull says I'm a saint,
> And they're both of them bound to be liars,
> For I'm neither of them, I ain't.
> I'm a man, and a man's a mixture,
> Right down from his very birth,
> For part of him comes from heaven,
> And part of him comes from earth.
> There's nothing in him that's perfect;
> There's nothing that's all complete.
> He's nobbut a great beginning
> From his head to the soles of his feet.

Every man well knows that he is a mixture. We know that we are capable at one time of an almost saintly goodness, and at another time of an almost devilish evil. We know that at one time we are capable of an almost sacrificial kindness, and at another of an almost heartless callousness. We know that sometimes the vision of goodness fills our horizon, and that other times the unclean and evil desire has us at its mercy. We are part ape and part angel.

There is clearly neither happiness or security in a life like that. There is continuous tension, continuous inner debate. A man is a walking civil war, never knowing which side within him will win the victory. Man as he is is a disintegrating personality and stands in need of integration. Clearly such integration can only come when some other force and power take possession of a man; something from outside him has to come in and take control; and that can only happen when a man can say what Paul said: "I live, yet not I, but Christ liveth in me" (Galatians 2. 20). Blessed indeed is the man who is at peace with himself, the man in whom the contradictions are obliterated, the man whose inner battle has been stilled in the control of Christ. Every man must long for peace in the inner warfare of his own personality and his own soul; and Jesus Christ is the only person who can make that peace.

There is a man's *relationship to his fellow-men*. Blessed is he who produces right relationships between man and man. There is little doubt that it is in this sense that a Jew would have taken this Beatitude, for, as we have already seen, to a Jew there were few higher achievements of this world than that of creating right relationships between men; and nothing is more necessary in this world than the creation of such relationships.

We live in a divided world with its iron curtains, its lines of demarcation, its divisions between race and race, nation and nation, and man and man. The strange Old Testament story regards this divided world as the curse of God upon man for man's overweening pride (Genesis 11. 1-9). It tells how men in their pride united to attempt to build a tower which would reach to heaven, and how God in punishment confounded and confused their languages so that they should be divided for ever after.

In the ancient world there was the division between Gentile and Jew. To this day if the son or daughter of a strictly orthodox Jewish family marries a Gentile, the family will carry out his funeral, for he is as one who is dead. In the ordinary form of morning prayer a Jew thanks God that God did not make him a Gentile, a slave or a woman. Even before God Jew and Gentile were separated. In the Temple in Jerusalem there were a series of Courts leading into the Holy Place. There was the Court of the Gentiles, the Court of the Women, the Court of the Israelites, and the Court of the Priests. Beyond the outer Court of the Gentiles the Gentile could not go. Between it and the Court of the Women there was a balustrade called the *Chel*. Inset at intervals along this balustrade there were stone tablets with the inscription on them: "No person of another race is to enter within the balustrade and embankment round the sacred place. Whoever is caught so doing will be answerable for his own death, which will follow." For the Gentile to seek the nearer presence of the God of the Jews was death.

In the Greek world there was what the Greeks called a "natural" division between Greek and barbarian, and by the word "natural" the Greek meant a barrier and a difference which was in the very course of nature, in the very structure of the world, something which must continue to be as long as the world should be. As Plato saw it, the barbarians were the natural enemies of the Greeks. Isocrates held that the greatness of Homer's poetry lay in the fact that it told of the wars of the Greeks against the barbarians, and held that Homer must always hold his place in the education of the young so that boys in every age might learn and imitate that ancient hatred. In the Greek Mystery Religions murderers and barbarians were classed together as being shut out; and all through this it must be remembered that a barbarian to the Greek was simply one who did not speak Greek.

In the modern world the divisions continue. There seems to be in the human mind an ineradicable suspicion of the stranger, so the suspicion of nation against nation continues. That suspicion is exacerbated when nations follow different philosophies of life, or when men are of different colours.

It is quite clear that a world like that cannot be other than a world which is both unhappy and unsafe. It is a world in which men must always be on guard, in which men must bend resources which could well have been devoted to better things to the purposes either of attack or self-defence, a world which may at any time erupt into a volcano of war and bloodshed. Aggrey of Africa did a great work as Principal of Achimoto College in West Africa. He died all too young, but he wrote his memory in the badge which he devised for the College. The badge was part of the keyboard of a piano with black and white notes. The symbolism is that some kind of music can no doubt be produced by using the white notes alone, or by using the black notes alone; but the best music can only be produced when black and white notes are used together in harmony. The danger of division is clear, and all man's troubled history is a demonstration of it; the desirability of unity is equally clear, as all men's prayers and visions combine to show. But the problem is where that unity is to find its source and its dynamic. The ancient Stoics believed that all men were born to be united, because that which gave all men life was that a spark of God had taken up its dwelling-place within their bodies. Men were men because they shared the common life of God, and, therefore, men should share all life together. Zeno, the founder of Stoicism, regarded the perfect state as a state which would include all men. In it a man would no longer say, " I am a citizen of Athens," but, " I am a citizen of the world." In the ideal state there would be no such thing as a lawcourt, for men would never dispute with one another. T. H. Robinson, commenting on this Beatitude says : " The ideal of God for human society is a spiritual condition in which jealousy, rivalry and hostility have disappeared, and a universal harmony prevails. He who is most worthy of congratulation for his true success in this difficult and complicated world of men and women is he who most perfectly succeeds in producing and upholding this harmony."

In no other power can this unity be found than in the power of Jesus Christ. There is abundant evidence that Jesus Christ can produce this unity. Bishop Lesslie Newbiggin tells of an experience in his diocese in India. When the United Church of South India came into being, and when he became one of its bishops, he made an introductory tour of his diocese. At each village the Christian community came out to meet its bishop. In one village the Christians were led by an extraordinary figure, clad in very aged R.A.F. equipment, and carrying a stainless steel baton. With this baton he controlled, as it were, his congregation. At a sign from him they knelt, and at another sign they rose. Bishop Newbiggin was staying with him when his story came out. His name was Sundaram. At the beginning of the second world war he was preaching the gospel in Burma. He was captured in the advance of the Japanese armies. He was taken to a guard-post. Everything he possessed was taken from him and he was bound and thrown into a corner. A Japanese officer came in. He went to the table where Sundaram's scanty belongings lay. He picked up the Tamil Bible. He knew no word of Tamil but he recognised it as a Bible. He held up his hand and traced on the palm the sign of the Cross and looked questioningly at Sundaram. Sundaram knew no word of Japanese, but he knew that the officer was asking if he was a Christian, and he nodded. The officer walked across to him, stood in front of him with his arms stretched out in the form of the Cross, cut his bonds, gave him back his belongings, and pointed to the door, bidding him to go. And, before Sundaram went out to freedom, the Japanese officer handed him as a token and memento his officer's staff; and that officer's staff was the stainless steel baton with which Sundaram directed his Indian congregation. Here were two men who knew not a word of each other's language, two men from nations which were at war, two men between whom there stretched a gulf which was humanly speaking beyond bridging—and Christ bridged that gulf. Jesus Christ reached out across the divisions and in Christ brought two men together again.

The phrase "Christ the Hope of the World" was never truer than it is to-day. If it were only possible that the Christian missionary might take the place of the invading army the peace of right relationships might yet come true in our time.

But the world in which we live has its divisions not only between nation and nation, but also between individual and individual. It is so often true that the human heart is the home of bitterness and of the unforgiving spirit. No one knew better than Jesus the tragedy of the jealousies and the envies and the bitternesses which separate man and man, for they invaded even the apostolic company. On the way to Jerusalem they were arguing among themselves about who should be greatest (Mark 9. 34). James and John came with their ambitious request for the principal places in the kingdom, and there was trouble among the Twelve (Mark 10. 35-45). Even at the Last Supper within the shadow of the Cross the Twelve were arguing about pre-eminence and about the first place (Luke 22. 24). Again, it is only Jesus Christ who can in himself create the right relationship between man and man. Bryan Greene talks of an incident in one of his American campaigns. At the end of the campaign he gathered a number of those who had shared in the campaign and who had found Christ, and asked them to state in one brief sentence without elaboration what the campaign had done for them and meant to them. There was a negro girl there. She had no difficulty in being brief, for she had no ability in words. She rose and she said: "Through this campaign I found Jesus Christ, and he made me able to forgive the man who murdered my father." *He made me able to forgive.* It is only when men enter into the right relationship with Jesus Christ that they can enter into the right relationship with each other.

Herein is part of the task of the Christian. The Christian must labour to produce right relationships between man and man. In any society, in the private society of a home, and in the public society of an institution or a Church, there are those who are disruptive influences and there are those who are reconciling influences. There are those who sow strife and there are those who sow peace. It must always be remembered that Christian reconciliation has a Godward and a manward look. It means the reconciliation of men to God and of men to each other; and there are few who are more blessed than those who produce and who maintain and who restore right relationships between man and man.

Man has a third relationship; he has a *relationship with God*. Man's relationship may be simply a consciousness of immense difference and infinite distance. It may be a relationship of fear and alienation in which a man tries to hide from God, as Adam did in the old story (Genesis 3. 8). It may be a relationship of enmity and hostility. Swinburne could speak of " the supreme evil—God ". It may be a relationship of complete indifference in which a man lives as if God did not exist. But it is easy to see the difference it must make to any man to see in the creator, the sustainer and the governor of the universe one in whose heart there is only love. Here again only Jesus Christ can produce that relationship. Whatever else is true of Jesus, this is certainly true, that in Jesus Christ we see perfectly displayed the attitude of

God to men; and when we realize that in Jesus Christ we see the Father (John 14. 9), that God is like Jesus, then there is born between us and God the new relationship in which, instead of avoiding his presence, we seek it, in which, instead of fleeing from him, we seek him, in which we find ourselves at home in the presence of God.

Blessed, indeed, is the man who breaks down the barriers between nation and nation, between man and man, and between man and God. Happy is the man whose life-work is the production of right relationships in ever sphere of life; and such relationships can only enrich life when a man's own relationship to Jesus Christ is right.

After the affirmation of the Beatitude there comes the promise. The peacemakers shall be called the children of God. The phrase " shall be called " is a Hebrew way of saying " shall be acknowledged to be ", or, " shall receive the status of ", or, " shall be owned and regarded as ". The peacemakers will enter into the honour of being the children of God. Further, the translation *children of God* is not quite accurate. It ought to be *sons of God,* and this in Hebrew has a special meaning. Hebrew is deficient in adjectives; there is, for instance, no adjective in the twenty-third psalm. To make up for this deficiency Hebrew uses the phrase *son of* plus some virtue or quality instead of an adjective. Barnabas, for instance, is the son of consolation; that is, he is a consoling and a comforting man. James and John are the sons of thunder; that is, they are thunderous and stormy characters. A man may be called a son of peace; that is, he is a peaceful and well-disposed man. So then the phrase "sons of God" means God-like. The translation of this Beatitude might well read: "Blessed are those who produce right relationships in every sphere of life, for they are doing a God-like work."

Repeatedly in the New Testament God is called the God of peace (Romans 15. 13; 16. 20; Philippians 4. 9; II Corinthians 13. 11; I Timothy 5. 23; Hebrews 13. 20, 21). God is the great establisher of right relationships; he gave his Son to establish and restore the right relationship between Himself and men; and, therefore, those who labour, toil and pray to bring right relationships between man and man and between man and God and between man and his own storm-tossed and divided heart can fitly be said to be God-like, and can fitly be said to be doing a God-like work. No man is more nearly kin to God than the man whose life is spent bringing peace among men, and no man's bliss is greater.

CHAPTER X

THE BLISS OF THE MARTYR'S PAIN

*Blessed are they which are persecuted for righteousness'
sake, for theirs is the kingdom of heaven.*

*Blessed are ye, when men shall revile you, and
persecute you, and shall say all manner of evil against
you falsely, for my sake.*

*Rejoice, and be exceeding glad, for great is your
reward in heaven; for so persecuted they the prophets
which were before you.* (MATTHEW 5. 10-12).

One of the most illuminating and significant facts about
the language of the early Church is that before the end
of the first century the word for *witness* and the word
for *martyr* had become the same Greek word. The
word is *martus;* its original meaning in ordinary Greek
is *witness;* but this is the word which came also to mean
martyr, because in that time the man who was a witness
had every chance of being a martyr too. There are,
indeed, times when we do not know which of the two
meanings of this Greek word the New Testament writers
would have had us to choose in translation. In the letter
to Smyrna John speaks of " Antipas my faithful *martus* "
(Revelation 2. 13); and we can equally well say that
Antipas was the faithful *witness* and the faithful *martyr*

97

of Christ, because for him, as for so many in these killing times, the one meaning implied the other. This is the Beatitude which tells of the bliss of the martyr's pain.

We must begin by thinking of the inevitability of persecution. There was in Jesus an almost startling honesty; no one could ever say that he had been induced to follow Jesus on false pretences; Jesus told his followers what they might expect, and he left them in no doubt that they must suffer for his name. To follow him necessarily involved the taking up of a cross (Matthew 16. 24). He had no doubt that his men would be brought before the magistrates, that they would be scourged in the Synagogues, and that they would be hated by all men because of their fidelity to him (Matthew 10. 16-22; Mark 13. 9; Luke 21. 17). The day would come when those who killed a Christian would think that they were rendering service to God (John 16. 2). They were not of the world as Jesus had not been of the world; and as the world had hated him, so it would necessarily hate them (John 15. 18, 19; 17. 14). The *world* in the Johannine sense of the term has been defined as " human nature organising itself without God ", and human nature apart from God must be in opposition to human nature which has taken God as the centre of existence. The day was to come when Peter, surely remembering this Beatitude, was to tell his people, who were going through it, that bliss was theirs, if they suffered, as Christ suffered, for righteousness' sake (I Peter 3. 14), and if they were reproached for the name of Christ (I Peter 4. 14). Jesus left his followers in no doubt of the cost of following him, and of the cross that loyalty to him involved.

What, then, were the reasons which from the heathen point of view made persecution inevitable?

There was the simple but basic fact that the Christians were different; and men always regard with suspicion that which is different. As far as the public is concerned, conformity is the way to a trouble-free life, and the Christians were inevitably non-conformists. "We have the reputation," said Tertullian, "of living aloof from crowds" (*Apology* 31). The Christians, as the heathen saw them, were people who "skulk in corners and shun the light of day, silent in public, but full of talk in their holes and corners", "people who separate themselves from the rest of mankind" (Minucius Felix, *Octavius* 8).

The difference of the Christian came out in all kinds of ways, and to this essential difference we will later return. The Christians had a completely different moral standard. Chastity was a new virtue, and a new demand. The Christian had perforce to abandon all social life. Every heathen meal began with a libation and a prayer to the pagan gods; in that a Christian could not share. Most heathen feasts and social parties were held in the precincts of a temple, after sacrifice had been made, and the invitation was usually the invitation to dine " at the table " of some god. To such a feast a Christian could not go. Inevitably the Christian seemed rude, boorish and discourteous when he refused the invitation to some social occasion. Even in the ordinary working life of the time the Christian was a problem. True, the Christian did not argue in favour of the emancipation of slaves, but he treated a slave as a brother, as, indeed, he believed him to be. Callistus, the third bishop of Rome, was a slave; he bitterly exacerbated heathen feeling by allowing marriage between high-born girls and freedmen who had been slaves, if both were Christian, and a marriage such as that was in the eyes of the Roman law quite illegal and no marriage at all. Roman civilisation was built on slavery and the Christians seemed to be undermining its very foundations. If a Christian was going to be strictly consistent and rigorous in his witness almost any trade was a danger. Clearly he could not be a gladiator or an actor; but even a mason might be involved in building the walls of a heathen temple, a tailor in making robes for a heathen priest, an incense-maker in making incense for the heathen sacrifices. Tertullian the rigorist even forbade a Christian to be a school teacher, because such teaching involved using as text-books the books which told the ancient stories of the gods, and observing the religious festivals of the pagan year. The Christian was almost bound to divorce himself from even the social and economic life of his time, and no man who divorces himself from his fellow-men in order to be better than his fellow-men can hope to be popular. The Christians were hated as men who seemed to wish to stand aloof from their fellow-men, and as men whose customs and way of life seemed likely to disrupt the social set-up of life.

At least some of the persecution directed against the Christians was connected with the Jews. The Jewish connection with persecution was twofold. First, since the early Christians at the beginning of the Church were almost all Jews, and since Christianity took its rise in Palestine, and since Jesus himself was a Jew, in its earliest days Christianity and Judaism were inextricably confounded in the heathen mind. To the heathen Christianity seemed to be a Jewish sect. Anti-semitism is no new thing, and in the ancient world the Jews were bitterly hated. All kinds of slanders about the Jews were prevalent. It was said that in the Holy of Holies there was an ass's head, because in the wilderness the Jews had been led by wild asses to water when they were perishing of thirst. Plutarch did not accept this story, but he suggested that the god of the Jews was the pig, because swine's flesh was sacred to them (Tacitus, *Histories* 5. 2-5; Plutarch, *Symposium* 4. 5; Juvenal, *Satires* 14. 96-106). The Jewish habit of observing the Sabbath gained them a reputation for idleness and laziness. "O Marcomanni, O Quadi, O Sarmatians," said Marcus Aurelius, "at last I have discovered a people more lazy than you" (*Ammianus Marcellinus* 22. 5). Worse than that, the rumour ran in Alexandria that once a year the Jews sacrificed a Gentile to their gods. It is true that the Jews were specially protected by the Romans, because, being the world's financiers and traders then as now, they were valuable members of the state. But every now and then there were popular bursts of violence against them, and they were always regarded with extreme dislike. Inevitably the Christians shared in this hatred, and inevitably the Christians were involved in the persecution which fell on the Jews at frequent intervals. Second, it is a fact that the Jews were behind at least some of the persecutions which fell upon the Christians. The Jews had access to the ear of those who were in authority. Their place in the business and commercial life of the world brought them into contact with the government and with the highest in the land. Very naturally they made every effort to dissociate themselves from the Christians and to make it clear that they had no connection with them; and often they used their influence to persuade the authorities to take action against the Christians. Around the Synagogue there gathered many Gentiles who were attracted by the Jewish belief in one God, and by the Jewish moral and ethical code, even if they were not prepared to accept circumcision and the whole Jewish law. In particular the moral teaching of Judaism was attractive to women. Many of the women who came to worship in the Synagogues were the wives of high government officials, and the Jews, as in Antioch (Acts 13. 50), did not hesitate to exert an influence against Christianity by persuading these women to persuade their husbands to put the law into action against the Christians. "The Synagogues," said Tertullian, "are the sources of persecution" (*Scorpiace* 10). Persecution came upon the Christians because in the popular mind they were confused with the Jews, and because the Jews used their widespread influence to foment persecution against them.

The Christians were accused of atheism. There were many among the heathen who could not understand an imageless worship, and for whom monotheism had no attraction. Even more serious, the Christians were accused of insulting the gods of the state. It is true that there was very little reality in the worship of the ancient gods by the time Christianity came to this world; but the worship of these old gods was still the state worship; it was part of a good citizen's duty to observe that worship: and the feeling was that, if that worship was not observed, the ancient gods took their revenge by sending disasters upon the state. The worship of the gods might be a convention, but it was a convention which for safety's sake had to be observed. So Tertullian writes: "If the Tiber floods the city, or if the Nile refuses to rise, or if the sky withholds its rain, if there is an earthquake, a famine, a pestilence, at once the cry is raised: 'The Christians to the lions.'" (Tertullian, *Apology* 40). Augustine tells us that in North Africa it has become a proverb, "If there is no rain, blame the Christians" (Augustine, *The City of God* 2. 3), and his greatest work *The City of God* is indeed designed to show that the sack of Rome in A.D. 410 was not due to the anger of the insulted and abandoned gods. It was easy and convenient to make the Christians the scapegoats for any disaster in the world.

One of the undeniable effects of Christianity was that it in fact did often make a division in the family. In that sense it was poignantly true that Christianity came not with peace but with a sword. An agonising situation was bound to arise when a son or a daughter became a Christian in defiance of the family, or when a husband and wife were divided by this new religion. It was literally true that Christianity could set a man at variance with his nearest and dearest, and that a man's foes could be those of this own household (Matthew 10. 34-37).

A Christian has to be prepared to love Christ more than he loved those who upon earth were closest to him. It was inevitable that the Christians should incur the charge of " tampering with family relationships ". Inevitably the heathen would hate this religion which disrupted their homes.

Even if the home was not disrupted, there were serious problems. A wife might become a Christian and a husband remain a pagan, and the two might still live together. But Tertullian tells us of the heathen husband who resented the fact that his wife " in order to visit the brethren goes from street to street to other men's houses, especially those of the poor. . . . He will not allow her to be present at all night long meetings and paschal solemnities. . . . He will not allow her to creep into prison to kiss a martyr's chains, or even to exchange the kiss of peace with one of the brethren " (Tertullian, *To his Wife* 2. 4. 5). One cannot but feel a certain amount of sympathy for the husband. It is clear that Christianity must often have produced a very difficult situation in many a home, and must in many cases have been heartily hated.

High on the list of things which brought hatred upon the Christians were the slanders which were disseminated about them, and which, once they were started, could not be halted. Mommsen writes: " The conviction that the Christian conventicles were orgies of lewdness, and receptacles of every crime, got hold on the popular mind with all the terrible vehemence of an aversion that resists all arguments and heeds not refutation." These slanders were accentuated by the secrecy of the Christian services, and especially by the fact that all who were not Christians were barred rigorously from the Sacrament. Secrecy always begets suspicion. The main slanders were three. The Christians were charged with cannibalism, a charge which came from the words of the Sacrament which speak of eating and drinking the body and the blood of Christ. They were charged with gross immorality, a charge which came from the fact that the Christian meeting was called the Agapē, the Love Feast, and from the custom of the kiss of peace, which the brethren gave to one another, and which, indeed, in the end became so liable to abuse that it was almost completely abandoned. It was alleged that the Christians killed and ate a child at their sacred meals. This may have been a reckless and a malicious allegation based on the fact that Christians were seen to carry children to the Christian meeting for baptism. It is not difficult to see how such charges could arise, and it is easy to see how the enemies of Christianity could use them as ammunition against the Christians, even if they knew them to be false, for there would be many who were more than willing to believe the worst.

We have not even yet come to the supreme cause of persecution. The supreme cause of persecution was the head-on clash between Christianity and Cæsar worship. Cæsar worship means the worship of the Roman Emperor as a god. Cæsar worship had a long history and a long development. In the great days of the Empire and of the Republic before it, the provincials did not resent the Roman sway; in many cases they welcomed it with wondering and heartfelt gratitude. There were even cases of kings voluntarily and of their own free will handing over and bequeathing their kingdoms to Rome. Rome brought to the world the *pax Romana,* the Roman peace. When the Romans took over the government of a country, impartial Roman justice arrived, and men were freed from the capricious government of unpredictable and often savage and bloodthirsty tyrants. When Roman administration came, the roads were cleared of brigands and the seas of pirates, and a new security entered into life. As E. J. Goodspeed put it: "The provincial, under Roman sway, found himself in a position to conduct his business, provide for his family, send his letters, and make his journeys in security, thanks to the strong hand of Rome." The result of this was a deep and heartfelt gratitude to the spirit of Rome. It was an easy step for the spirit of Rome to become the goddess Roma, and by the second century B.C. there were many temples in Asia Minor to the goddess Roma. But the human mind and heart characteristically need a symbol; it was a further easy step to see the goddess Roma and the spirit of Rome incarnated in the Emperor. He embodied Rome; he was Rome; in him the spirit of Rome resided and had its earthly dwelling. The first temple actually built to the godhead of the Emperor was built in Pergamum in 29 B.C.

So far the worship of Rome and of the Emperor was a quite spontaneous growth, not in any way imposed upon the people. At first the Emporors were very hesitant about this. Claudius refused to have temples erected to him because, as he said, he did not wish to be offensive to his fellow-men. But slowly an idea began to dawn and form in the official mind. The problem of the Roman Empire was the problem of unification. The Empire stretched from the river Euphrates and beyond it to Britain and the shores of the Irish sea. It stretched from Germany to North Africa, from Spain to Egypt. Here were all kinds of peoples, and languages, and faiths, and traditions. How could they be welded into a unity? How could there be brought into their lives the consciousness of being one empire? There is no unifying force like the force of a common religion; and Cæsar worship lay ready to hand. None of the local and ancestral faiths had any hope of ever becoming universal, but Rome was universal. The result was, as W. M. Ramsay says, that Cæsar worship became "the keystone" of imperial policy. It was deliberately universalised; it was deliberately organised in every province in the Empire. Everywhere temples to the godhead of the Emperor were erected. It was precisely the cost of the administration of Caesar worship in the Roman temple in the city which is now Colchester that provided the tragic and disastrous revolt of Boadicea in Britain in A.D. 61

There was another step to be taken—and it was taken. Cæsar worship was made universal—and it was made compulsory for every race and nation within the Empire with the single exception of the Jews. On a certain day in the year every Roman citizen had to come to the Temple of Cæsar and had to burn a pinch of incense there, and say: "Cæsar is Lord." When he had done that, he was given a certificate to certify that he had done so, and that certificate he had to get.

We must note one thing. The Romans were the reverse of intolerant; they were the most tolerant masters the world has ever seen. After a man had burned his pinch of incense and had acknowledged Cæsar as Lord, he could go away and worship any god he liked, so long as the worship did not affect public decency and public order. It can be seen at once that Cæsar worship was first and foremost a test of political loyalty; it was a test of whether or not a man was a good citizen; and, if a man refused to carry out the ceremony of acknowledging Cæsar, he was automatically branded as a traitor and a revolutionary and a disloyal and disaffected citizen.

It was here that Christianity and Cæsar worship met in head-on collision. The one thing which no Christian would ever say was: "Cæsar is Lord." For the Christian Jesus Christ and Jesus Christ alone was Lord. To the Roman the Christian seemed utterly intolerant and insanely stubborn; worse, he seemed a self-admittedly disloyal citizen. Had the Christians been willing to burn that pinch of incense and to say formally, "Cæsar is Lord," they could have gone on worshipping Christ to their heart's content; but the Christians would not compromise. Rome regarded them as a band of potential revolutionaries threatening the very being of the Empire; and Rome struck and struck again.

It was not that persecution was constant and consistent. For long periods the Christians were left in peace. But like a sword of Damocles persecution was always poised above them. It only took a malicious informer, a popular demand, a governor determined to carry out the letter of the law, and the storm would burst. The Christian as a Christian was legally an outlaw. "Public hatred," says Tertullian, "asks but one thing, and that not investigating into the crimes charged, but simply the confession of the Christian name" (Tertullian, *Apology* 2).

So we see that Jewish malevolence, popular slander and dislike, and political principles all converged to make the persecution of the Christians inevitable. A Christian, as a Christian, was regarded as the enemy of the state, as a public enemy, an outlaw.

When we look at the experiences of the persecuted, we see even more vividly the amazing paradox which this Beatitude contains when it speaks of the bliss of the martyr's pain. The persecution of the Christians took more than one form. At its mildest it would involve social ostracism; the Christian would inevitably become an outsider, to whom the doors once open would now be shut. The Christian, as we have seen, would have to face a constant campaign of slander. The First Epistle of Peter more than once speaks of those who speak evil against the Christians (I Peter 2. 12; 3. 16). The Christian day by day lived in a society in which the most slanderous tales were whispered, and even shouted from the house-tops, against him. There were times when this pagan suspicion and dislike erupted in an outbreak of looting and destruction and mob violence. The Letter to the Hebrews tells how the Christians have uncomplainingly accepted the spoiling of their goods (Hebrews 10. 34). But it is when we see the sadistic and savage ingenuity of the punishment inflicted on the Christians in the official persecutions that we see what persecution really meant. H. B. Workman in *Persecution in the Early Church* has a summary of the terrors which the Christians had to face. "If," he writes, "we confine ourselves to strictly historical cases, the savagery, though to a large extent part of the judicial process of the age, is appalling. Some, suffering the punishment of parricides, were shut up in a sack with snakes and thrown into the sea; others were tied to huge stones and cast into a river. For Christians the cross itself was not deemed sufficient agony; hanging on trees, they were beaten with rods until their bowels gushed out, while vinegar and salt were rubbed into their wounds. In the Thebias, during the persecution of Diocletian, Christians were tied to catapults, and so wrenched limb from limb. Some, like Ignatius, were thrown to the beasts; other tied to their horns. Women were stripped, enclosed in nets, and exposed to the attacks of furious bulls. Many were ' made to lie on sharp shells ', and tortured with scrapers, claws and pincers before being delivered to the mercy of the flames. Not a few were broken on the wheel, or torn in pieces by wild horses. Of some the feet were slowly burned away, cold water being poured over them the while lest the victims should expire too rapidly. Peter, one of the servants of Diocletian, was scourged to the bone, then placed near a gridiron that he might witness the roasting of pieces of flesh torn from his own body. At Lyons they tried to overcome the obstinacy of Sanctus of Vienne ' by fixing red-hot plates to the most delicate parts of his body '. Down the backs of others 'melted lead, hissing and bubbling,' was poured; while a few, by the clemency of the Emperor, escaped with the searing out of their eyes, or the tearing off of their legs . . . . to say nothing of the rack, the hobby-horse, the claws, and other tortures preparatory to sentence."

These are not pretty or pleasant experiences to visualise, but it is well to remember that Christianity both in the human and the divine sense is a blood-bought faith.

Let us briefly return again to the reasons for this persecution. We have already seen how the political demand of Cæsar worship dominated the situation; but that demand for persecution on the part of the authorities could hardly have succeeded and could hardly have been continued, unless it had had, at least to some extent, public opinion behind it.

The main cause of the hatred of the Christians was the fact that they were different. The word which is used to describe the Christian in the New Testament itself is intensely significant. It is the word *hagios;* that is the word which is so often translated *saints.* It is also the word whose standard meaning is *holy.* The root meaning of this word is *different.* That which is *hagios,* holy, is different from other things. The Temple is holy because it is different from other buildings; the Sabbath day is holy because it is different from other days. The Christian is, therefore, a person who is fundamentally *different.* Now, if that difference had been expressed by withdrawal from life, there might well have been dislike, but it is improbable that the dislike would have issued in persecution. But the Christian difference was a difference which was expressed within the world. Paul does not write to the saints in the desert, or to the saints in a monastery; he writes to the saints in Philippi and in Rome. It was, therefore, inevitable that the Christians daily confronted the heathen with this difference in their lives.

Further, the difference which was expressed in the life of the Christian was a difference which was a constant unspoken criticism and condemnation of the pagan way of life. It was not that the Christian went about criticising and condemning and disapproving; nor was it that the Christian was consciously self-righteous and superior. It was simply that the Christian ethic in itself was a criticism and condemnation of pagan life and standards. People will always seek to eliminate that which silently condemns them. One of the most famous of all early Athenian statesmen was Aristides, who was called the Just. In the end he was banished, not for any crime, but simply because the people were humiliated and abased at the sight of the goodness of the man. Plutarch tells of the time when the people were voting on whether or not he was to be banished. Those who voted for his banishment had to write his name on an *ostracon,* a piece of pottery. An illiterate fellow, who did not know Aristides even by sight, approached Aristides himself, and, being unable to write, asked him to write *Aristides* on the *ostracon* and so to enable him to record his vote for banishment. Aristides asked him if Aristides had ever done him an injury which made him vote for his banishment. "None at all," said the man. "I do not even know this man; but I am tired of hearing him everywhere called the Just." The existence of a just man was in itself an offence. There was a surprising friendship between Alcibiades, the brilliant but debauched young Athenian, and Socrates. But sometimes Alcibiades would say to Socrates: "Socrates, I hate you; for when I am with you I realize what I am."

The Christians were persecuted because the difference in their lives was a daily rebuke to many of the pagans. Peter says that the heathen spoke evil of the Christians for no other reason than that the Christians did not run with them to the same excess of riot (I Peter 4. 4). It is an abiding fact in the human situation that the Christian will always be liable to persecution of one kind or another for the reason that the Christian is bound to be the conscience of whatever community of which he may be a member. The Christian does not even need to speak; his presence and his life are a conscience to the sphere, the society, the circle in which he moves. It is not a matter of spoken criticism and constant fault-finding; it is not a matter of conscious superiority; it is simply that the existence of the Christian life is a reminder of what life ought to be and a condemnation of the world as it is. It is no new thing for a man to seek to silence his conscience. The Christian as the conscience of the community must be exposed to the dislike, the hatred, and the attack of that part of the world which lives without God.

What, then, is the Christian defence against this persecution and this attack? It is a notable and an extremely important and significant fact that in the great early days of the Church the Christian never conceived of the possibility of using force to meet persecution. It was not long before the Christians were so numerous that concerted Christian action might well have overturned the Roman government. But the Christian did not believe that Christianity could be defended by the use of any kind of force. Against persecution the Christian had two weapons. First, he had the weapon of the Christian life. It is the appeal of Peter that the Christians should silence the slanders of the world by living so finely that these slanders should be demonstrated to be untrue. The Christian must show himself so loyal and so useful a citizen, and so good and so conscientious a servant, that the slanders of the heathen should be silenced (I Peter 2. 12-18). The Christian must have so good a conscience that he will put to shame those who make any accusation against him (I Peter 3. 13-16). In the days of persecution the Church grasped one great principle which remains for ever valid and true—the only effective Christian propaganda is the propaganda of a good life; the only defence of Christianity is the Christian. Second, the Christian had the defence of Christian apologetic. It was Peter's insistence that the Christian must ever be ready to give an answer to any man who asks him a reason for the hope that is in him (I Peter 3. 15). That is to say, if the Christian is to meet an attack on the Christian faith, he must know what he believes and why he believes it.

The only weapons which the Christian can use against any kind of persecution are the demonstration of the Christian life, and the intelligent presentation of the Christian belief.

In regard to persecution we have one question still left to ask. How can we speak of the blessedness of the persecuted? How can we speak of the bliss of the martyr's pain? On the face of it it seems strange and contradictory and paradoxical, and yet, when we come to think about it, it is not difficult to see that there is a joy in persecution, a joy which is specifically the martyr's joy.

Persecution is in fact a compliment. To persecute a person is to show that we take him so seriously that we consider that he must be eliminated. No one will persecute a person who is futile, ineffective, and indecisive. Persecution only comes to the man whose life is so positive and real in its effectiveness that society regards him as a danger. George Bernard Shaw said that the finest compliment the world can pay an author is to burn his books, because the world thereby shows that it regards these books as so dynamic and explosive that they cannot be allowed to continue to affect the minds of men. Persecution is always a proof of the utter genuineness and sincerity of the faith of the man who is persecuted. A time-serving, compromising, facing-both-ways, hypocritical, uncommitted Christian will never be persecuted. To be persecuted is to be complimented as a real Christian.

Persecution is an opportunity to demonstrate loyalty. It is when things become difficult that there comes the acid test of the loyalty of the Christian. Persecution gives to the Christian the opportunity to show that he is not ashamed of the gospel of Christ, and that he does not shrink from showing whose he is and whom he serves.

To be persecuted is to walk in the way of the saints, the prophets and the martyrs. " So persecuted they the prophets which were before you " (Matthew 5. 12). To be amongst the persecuted is to have the thrill of knowing that we are one of the great company of those whose names are on the honour-roll of the faith.

To endure persecution is undoubtedly the way to satisfaction. Time and time again the verdict of history is with the persecuted and not the persecutor. James Russell Lowell, the American poet, wrote in his poem called *The Present Crisis*:

> Truth for ever on the scaffold, Wrong for ever
>   on the throne,
> Yet that scaffold sways the future, and, behind
>   the dim unknown,
> Standeth God within the shadow, keeping
>   watch above His own.

But—and it can be even more important—the brave and loyal acceptance of persecution enables a man to meet his own verdict upon his own self. The Stoics used to argue that in the last analysis a man instinctively knows and admits that he would rather do the right and accept persecution than do the wrong and escape persecution. They use a famous illustration. In Greek history there were two famous men called Harmodius and Aristo-geiton who plotted and planned against tyranny and for freedom. Their plan was discovered; they were arrested and killed. Both of them had been friendly with a famous Athenian courtesan, an *hetaira,* called Laeaena, which means Lioness. After the arrest and death of Harmodius and Aristogeiton Laeaena too was arrested, and every effort was made to compel her to divulge the names of others who were implicated in the plot. Laeaena was so determined to keep faith with her former friends and clients that under torture she deliberately bit out her tongue, lest she should speak. So in memory of her the Athenians erected a famous bronze statue of a tongueless lioness. The Stoics posed the question, Whether would you rather be Laeaena in the days of her luxury and her pleasure and her cushioned ease, or in the hour when she bit out her tongue rather than be disloyal to those who had called her friend? There is no doubt as to the answer to that question. Instinctively the heart of man sides with Laeaena in her torture.

The history of the Church of England has an outstanding example of this principle in action. Thomas Cranmer was archbishop of Canterbury; he had leanings towards Protestantism and he was closely affiliated to the Protestants. When Mary came to the throne, and began her persecuting career in her attempt to obliterate Protestantism, Cranmer was arrested. Thereupon to save his life he signed no fewer than six recantations of all his connection with Protestantism. His recantations did not in the end succeed in saving his life; but when the time came to die, Cranmer found a new courage. In St. Mary's Church in Oxford he was brought forward to repeat his recantations. Instead of doing so he ended his address to the deeply moved congregation: "Now I come to the great thing that troubleth my conscience more than any other thing I said or did in my life, and that is the setting abroad of writings contrary to the truth, which here I now renounce and refuse as things written by my hand contrary to the truth I thought in my heart, and written for fear of death to save my life, if it might be. And forasmuch as my hand offended in writing contrary to my heart, my hand, therefore, shall be the first punished; for, if I come to the fire, it shall be the first burned." And, when he did come to the stake, he held out his hand and put it into the flames saying: "This was the hand that wrote it, therefore, it shall suffer first punishment." And, holding it steadily in the flames, " he never stirred nor cried till life was gone." For Cranmer the joy of martyrdom was far greater than the joy of escape. To evade persecution may be to escape trouble for the moment, but in the end it is to beget that self-contempt which makes life intolerable. To face persecution may bring the agony of the moment, but in the end it is the way to satisfaction and to peace of heart.

All through the New Testament there runs the conviction that to accept and to endure persecution places a man in a special relationship with Jesus Christ. To accept undeserved suffering and persecution is to follow the example of Christ and to walk in His steps (I Peter 2. 21-24). The suffering which faith and loyalty bring is for his sake (Philippians 1. 29). In this connection the thought of the New Testament can be very bold. To suffer for the faith is to be a partaker, a sharer, in the sufferings of Jesus Christ (I Peter 4. 13-16). It is in Paul that we find the greatest thought of all. To suffer for the faith is to "fill up that which is behind of the afflictions of Christ" (Colossians 1. 24). It is as if that when the Christian suffers, he suffers that which is lacking in the sufferings of Christ, as if he completed the full total of the sufferings of Christ. What can that mean? How can there be anything incomplete or lacking in the sufferings of Christ?

When some great discovery which affects the health and the welfare of man has been made by a scientist in his laboratory, or by a doctor in his surgery, it has still to be made available to men and women in general. The discovery is itself only half the battle; the making of it available is just as important; and it often happens that the making of it available involves a long battle with ignorance and prejudice and hostility and opposition. It has often happened that the cost of making some discovery available was greater than the cost of the initial discovery. Here we have an analogy to the position of the work of Christ and of our share in it. The Christ-deed is completed and done; the Cross is endured and the victory is won. But the news of what Christ did, and the offer of salvation in Christ has still to be brought to all men. The bringing of that news can be costly. It can involve sacrifice and suffering and martyrdom and death; and all that suffering can in a real sense be said to be the completing of the suffering of Christ, for without it the sacrifice of Christ can never be known to men. Further, Jesus Christ lived and died to make this world a certain kind of world for men and women; he lived and died that men and women everywhere should not only know salvation and the forgiveness of sins and peace with God, but also that they should live a life of health and happiness and liberty and freedom such as befits sons and daughters of God to live. It has cost many and many a sacrifice, and it will continue so to do, to make the kind of society and the kind of world to which the name Christian can be given; but such a world and such a society were the aim of Christ, and he who toils and labours and suffers and endures to make such a world is in a real sense sharing in filling up and completing the sufferings of Jesus Christ. The greatest thought of all is that he who suffers for the faith and for the betterment of the men and women for whom Christ died is a sharer in the sufferings of Christ and is even filling up that which is still lacking in the sufferings of his Lord.

The ultimate reward of such suffering is clear. Jesus Christ will be in no man's debt. He who is partaker in the sufferings of Christ will inevitably share in the glory of Christ. If we suffer with him, we shall be glorified with him (Romans 8. 17). To be partakers of the suffering is to be partakers of the consolation (II Corinthians 1. 7). If we suffer with him, we shall also reign with him (II Timothy 2. 12). The essence of Christianity is union with Christ, and that union will necessarily involve union with his sufferings and union with his glory.

THE EPILOGUE

We have studied and thought our way through the Beatitudes and now there remain two things to say. One of them is a warning, and the other is an encouragement.

i. Let us begin with the warning. It is to be noted to whom the Beatitudes and the whole Sermon on the Mount are addressed. They are addressed to the *disciples* (Matthew 5. 1). That is to say, the Beatitudes and the Sermon on the Mount describe a way of life which is only addressed to, and only possible for, the committed Christian.

We frequently hear people saying that the world would enter into a new and perfect age of peace and love, if only people would live according to the teaching of the Beatitudes and of the Sermon on the Mount. Lionel Curtis insists that the Church must never be regarded as an end in itself, but as the means and instrument towards what he calls the realization of the Commonwealth of God upon earth. He goes on to say that, if he is asked to define what he means by that Commonwealth, his answer is: "The Sermon on the Mount reduced to political terms." The way to the perfect world is the acceptance and the living of the teaching of the Sermon on the Mount.

The next step taken by so many is to say: "Let us have the Christian ethic without minding about the

Christian theology. Let us have the ethic without bothering about the religion. Let us have the ethic without thinking about who Jesus was, or about the claims which he made upon men."

The answer to this is that the Christian ethic is only possible for the committed Christian. The proof of that statement is obvious. The world has had the Sermon on the Mount and the Christian ethic clear before it for almost two thousand years and it is no nearer to achieving it and working it out in practice. It still remains a dream and a vision. The plain truth is that the Christian ethic is completely impossible without the Christian dynamic.

There is in this world an obvious difference between *ought* and *can*. There is all the difference in the world between what a man ought to do in theory and what he can do in fact. It may be perfectly correct to say to a fat, flabby, out of condition, middle-aged man that he *ought* to be able to run the hundred yards race in ten seconds, but the plain fact is that he cannot do so. When we think of a world in terms of men and women living and acting towards each other on the basis of the Sermon on the Mount, the whole dream is a complete impossibility without that committal to Jesus Christ from which the ability to live this kind of life springs. Only he who gave us his commands can enable us to obey these commands. The Christian ethic is a complete impossibility without Christ. There is no such thing in this world as Christian power and Christian living without Christian commitment. It is not the Christian ethic which makes Christian men and women; it is Christian men and women who can live the Christian ethic. The Sermon on the Mount, the essence of the Christian ethic, was addressed to those who were disciples; and the Christian ethic can never be divorced from commitment to Jesus Christ.

ii. But there is also encouragement here. The disciples were disciples before Jesus taught them. They had not waited to understand everything before they linked their lives to the life of Jesus Christ. They linked their lives to him and then he taught them.

There are many people who refuse to commit themselves to Jesus Christ and to his Church because they do not understand this or that doctrine, or because there are certain things in Christianity which are a mystery to them. There is no one in this world who understands the whole of Christianity. G. K. Chesterton said long ago that only the fool tries to get the heavens into his head, in which case his head not unnaturally bursts; the Christian man and the wise man is quite content to get his head inside the heavens.

Once Jesus said a very relevant thing. "If any man will do his will, he shall know of the doctrine" (John 7. 17). If we start out on the Christian way, even if we are well aware that our understanding of the Christian doctrine is very imperfect and very inadequate, it will become clearer to us the more we do the will of God as we know it. The old Latin tag has it: *Solvitur ambulando*. The problems clear up as we go ahead. The man who waits to understand everything will wait for ever. We must begin with what we know and as we go on we will understand more and more.

The ideal is there. The way to the ideal is committal to Jesus Christ; and for that committal we do not need to wait for perfect understanding; we can begin with love.